KIRK LORE

Answers to
Some Interesting Questions
on the Constitution and History
of the Kirk in Scotland

ANDREW HERRON

SAINT ANDREW PRESS
EDINBURGH

First published in 1999 by
SAINT ANDREW PRESS
121 George Street, Edinburgh EH2 4YN

ISBN 0 7152 0772 5

British Library Cataloguing in Publication Data

A catalogue record for
this book is available
from the British Library

ISBN 0715207725

This book has been set in Bembo and Charlemagne.

Cover design by Mark Blackadder.
Illustrations adapted from Revd J A Wylie (ed): *The Scots Worthies:
Their Lives and Testimonies* (Wm Mackenzie & Co: London, *c.* 1880).
Typesetting by Lesley A Taylor.
Printed and bound by Bell and Bain Ltd, Glasgow.

CONTENTS

THEME V – The MINISTRY

THEME VI – MACHINERY of ADMINISTRATION

THEME VII – The RIGHT to DIFFER

FOREWORD

by Ronald S Blakey

A NINETIETH birthday is obvious cause for
congratulations, cordial reminiscence and the
giving of gifts. Congratulating Andrew Herron
on attaining this milestone is made all the more
pleasurable by the fact that it is he who gives us
the gift in these refreshingly readable glimpses of
Scottish Church History, all wrapped and laced
in the style he has made his own.

The more seasoned reader will instantly
recognise those questions from an earlier day that
Andrew addresses and will welcome his easy
clarity of language which jogs the memory and
makes good some gaps in a knowledge which has
probably always been less perfect than we like to
pretend. The younger reader will learn a great
deal very quickly about the Church of today and
at the same time be transported back to a Scotland where, for a mix of reasons good and ill,
the exploits of the Church were regularly head-
line news.

An appreciation of our past can explain some
of our Church's present strengths and even
excuse, in part, some of its current weaknesses.
Above all, it can deepen our resolve that the
Andrew Herron of the next ninety years, should
our Church be so fortunate as to have anyone
worthy of such an accolade, will find as much to
admire and inspire in us as there has been in the
faith of our forefathers.

September 1999

GOVERNMENT
BY COURTS

UNTIL the time of the Reformation all government, alike in State and Church, was monarchical in character. The King (or Pope) sat on the Throne of State (or of St Peter) and power and responsibility came down in ever-widening circles therefrom.

It is truly remarkable that the Scottish Reformers, when they came to devise a constitution for the Kirk, should have avoided adopting some modification of this pattern. Instead they created a completely new system based on the conciliar principle where courts or councils take the place of individuals, where the hierarchy instead of being of individuals is of courts with the lowest of these enjoying considerable power and initiative. This clearly is not democracy as we understand it today, but it is as far a cry from the 'divine right of kings' as it is from 'the historic episcopate'. It certainly amounts to what in its day must have been a quite revolutionary change.

When first established the system was not, naturally, worked out with the completeness that we know today, but from the very outset it represented a model designed to maintain a Kirk by divine right. It was to lead to much bitter struggle, but in the end it emerged as what is probably the most perfect pattern of Church-State relationship known anywhere. It represents also a pattern well suited to the genius of the Scottish people.

1
WHAT IS
A KIRK SESSION?

WHEN, in the mid-sixteenth century, the leaders of the Scottish Reformation faced up to the task of designing a system of Church government, their basic aims were clear: to secure that the services of a National Kirk would be available in every corner of the land, providing a spiritual health service, maintaining the moral condition of society, and securing a measure of education for all. Their Scotland was vastly different from what we know today – sparsely populated, its economy wholly rural, with few considerable centres of population, but with a natural division into parishes.

What more natural, then, than that they should adopt this ready-to-hand unit, the parish, as the bottom line of their structure. In every parish there would be a Kirk with a resident Minister; there would also be a school and a dominie, for if people were to acquire a saving knowledge of Scripture they had to be able to read their Bibles. And there would be a Kirk Session to maintain spiritual oversight over the whole affair.

Many things have changed, some fairly radically, in these four centuries, but the conception of the Kirk Session, its constitution and its duties, has not changed, except that since 1966 women have been eligible for ordination as Elders on the same terms as men.

Its Constitution

A Kirk Session cannot function without a Minister as Moderator – either the Minister of the parish or, the charge being vacant or its Minister absent on leave, another Minister appointed by the Presbytery as Moderator *ad interim*, or in certain emergencies and for strictly limited business, another Minister as Moderator *pro tempore*. Meetings are normally called by the Moderator when he deems it expedient, though today it is usual for Sessions to meet on regular occasions. There is provision for a meeting being requisitioned by more than a third of the Elders. The Minister cannot as Moderator propose a motion and his only vote is a casting one.

The Kirk Session is a highly independent and autonomous body. It decides when it wants to add to its own number and who these shall be. Even when it asks the Congregation to elect, it is the Kirk Session that takes the final step of approving the choice and then of ordaining and admitting.

Its meetings are in private, unless for some special reason it decides otherwise. It does not take instruction from nor is it accountable to the congregation. In all things it is answerable to the Presbytery of the bounds and ultimately to the Assembly. There is, of course, nothing to prevent it – and in many cases much to commend it – taking the congregation into its confidence on some major issue, especially where large sums of money are at stake.

Its Duties

The duties of the Kirk Session are to maintain good order, to cause Acts of Assembly to be put in execution, to administer discipline, to judge and determine cases, and to superintend the moral and spiritual condition of the parish. It fixes the hours of public worship and the number of services, appoints and provides for the administration of Baptism and for the observance of the Lord's Supper. By long-standing tradition the Elders assist the Minister at the latter, but Communion is not a Session affair and the court need not be constituted.

It has no voice in the matter of worship, responsibility for which lies ultimately with the

Presbytery, of which the Minister acts as the executive officer.

First communicants have to be approved by the Kirk Session which resolves to admit and add their names to the Roll, and this it has to revise and attest each year. By dividing the parish into Districts and setting an Elder in charge of each, most Kirk Sessions today seek to fulfil their duty of spiritual oversight. When the congregation falls vacant, the Session has to prepare an Electoral Register, to arrange for an election once a nominee has been chosen, and to declare the result.

Session and Discipline

In the exercise of discipline a wide gulf separates the Kirk Session of today from its counterpart of yesteryear. As is well known to every student of Scottish life and manners, the Session of an earlier day took a most lively interest in the private life and behaviour of everyone in the parish and was not slow to summon people to give an account of their behaviour were the faintest breath of scandal to arise. For this they have been criticised – unfairly I think. They were wrong, certainly in imagining that people could be obliged to be good by such methods, but I think they fulfilled what they saw to be their duty with as little sense of personal gratification as the magistrate of today, and I should say from what I have read that they sought to be scrupulously fair. Having no effective sanctions with which to follow up its judgments, today's Session must find a more positive approach if it is to win people from evil and scandalous courses.

The Kirk Session of early times had a most onerous and important function in caring for the poor, a duty of which today's Session is mercifully relieved.

2
WHAT IS
A PRESBYTERY?

IT is odd that the Presbytery, which in a quite real sense has become the basic court of the Church, should have emerged as a kind of after-thought. The original framework provided for only 'congregational, provincial, and national assemblies' – that is to say, Kirk Session, Synod and General Assembly. As early as 1581, however, Presbyteries were established, and from the very outset they began to take over more and more of the functions of the Provincial Synod until today that court has been abolished altogether.

The Kirk Session rules a geographical area. In the same way the Presbytery is set over the territory 'within its bounds', including all the congregations within that area. It has too a regular place of meeting – its 'seat' – and while it may convene at different places within its bounds for inductions and such-like functions (meeting *in hunc effectum*), it normally meets for the trans-action of ordinary business at its seat.

A peculiarity of the Presbytery is that it must always be either 'in session' or else 'appointed to meet pursuant to adjournment'. Before rising it must always appoint, and make public intimation of its next sederunt. In circumstances of urgency the Moderator may call a special meeting (*pro re nata*), the first item of business at such a gather-ing being the ratification of the Moderator's conduct, and the emergency item being the only piece of competent business.

Unique Status

The importance of these provisions governing the regularity and public character of the Presbytery's doings stem from the fact that it is a court of the land and all citizens should know how to gain access to it. In the words of Lord President Inglis the Presbytery is 'an established judicature of the country and as such recognised by law as the Court of Session itself'.

That too is why the Presbytery is always an open court, meeting in public unless for some particular item of business it resolves to meet 'alone' or 'behind closed doors'. In dealing with any matter of a judicial character the Presbytery must proceed with circumspection, for its judgments cannot be made the subject of appeal to a civil court. Lord Justice Clerk Moncreiff states:

> *The jurisdiction of the Church courts ... rests upon a similar statutory foundation to that under which we administer justice within these walls. As this is a matter ... solely within the cognizance of the Church courts I think we have no power whatever to interfere.*

Its Membership

The Presbytery consists of Ministers and Elders in more or less equal numbers and also, since 1991, of members of the Diaconate employed within the bounds. It includes every Minister of a charge along with an Elder, elected for a year at a time by each Kirk Session (even although linked), and also a number of additional Ministers – retired, employed in the Divinity Faculties, chaplains of various sorts, ordained assistants as well as a number of Elders appointed by the Presbytery at its own will.

One of the ministerial members is chosen by free election to act as Moderator – for a year at a time. An Act of 1996 made it legal for an Elder or Deacon to hold this office.

A Clerk is appointed (who need not be a member of the court) officially to keep a record of proceedings, though many other duties are likely to devolve upon him or her. In the absence of either Moderator or Clerk, an appointment must be made *pro tempore* before any business may be transacted.

Its Size

At the beginning of the century it was reported there were 84 Presbyteries; one including five parishes, one 94. Over the years, with depopulation on one side and improved communications on the other, adjustments have taken place. Following on regionalisation in 1974 a massive review of Presbytery bounds was undertaken to make them conform roughly with those of the new Districts. Today there are in Scotland 46 Presbyteries, one having nine parishes (Uist), and another 156. In the case of the large Presbytery (Glasgow) there are 99 Ministers over and above those in parishes, so that the total ministerial strength, were there no vacancies, would be exactly 255. There are also Diaconal members. Certainly some Presbyteries are too small while others suffer from the opposite complaint. The trouble is that Uist is a unit which cannot realistically be increased while the City of Glasgow with its suburban outreach is likewise a unit which cannot realistically be reduced or divided.

Its Duties

The duties of the Presbytery were in 1592 defined by an Act of the Scottish Parliament as: 'to see that the Word of God is purely preached within its bounds, the Sacraments rightly administered, and the discipline intertenyit'. Though in detail, and even more in emphasis, the work of the Presbytery has altered greatly in the intervening centuries, this basic statement is still sound.

It is the business of the Presbytery of today:

- to maintain and enforce existing law and usage in the matter of public worship;
- to supervise the conduct of Ministers in their professional capacity, with power, if required, to libel, try, and sentence them;
- to ensure that the orders of superior courts are observed;
- to make rules for good order within congregations;
- to nominate, oversee, and licence students of divinity;
- to ensure that vacancy business is properly conducted, to satisfy itself regarding the election of a Minister, and in due course to induct him;
- to be a court of appeal from Kirk Sessions;
- to consider questions of readjustment of congregations, and to delimit parishes.

The Presbytery also appoints each year the Minister and Elders who will be its commissioners to the General Assembly.

3
WHAT IS
THE DIACONATE?

THE roots of the term 'Deacon' lie deep in Scripture, but the branches have spread in a variety of directions.

In the bad old days when it was firmly held that a woman should not raise her voice in any public place, the Kirk was far-seeing enough to recognise the fair sex had a unique contribution which they could offer to the work of Christ and that there were many highly gifted ladies willing and indeed keen to serve in some capacity.

It was as comparatively recently as 1888, however, that legislation appeared regarding the office of Deaconess, how applicants were to be chosen and set apart, the duties they might perform, and so on. In the Free Church it would seem there were two 'levels' – the Church Sister and the Deaconess, the latter involving 'a higher educational standard, administrative ability and responsibility, leadership in Home Mission work in connection with a congregation, Presbytery or Committee of the Church'.

All members of the Diaconate are now members of the Presbytery in which they are working and may be corresponding members of their Kirk Sessions (Act III 1992). They may be sent as commissioners to the General Assembly.

4
WHAT WAS
A SYNOD?

THE Assembly of 1992 enacted as follows:

The General Assembly, with the consent of no less than two-thirds of the whole of the Presbyteries of the Church, gained in two immediately successive years, enact, ordain and declare that Provincial Synods shall be abolished, and accordingly that Article II of the Articles Declaratory of the Constitution of the Church of Scotland in Matters Spiritual (1921) shall be amended by the deletion of the words Provincial Synods with effect from 1st January 1993.

So the Synod is no more: but let us glance at what it was and find the reasons for its demise.

As the Kirk Session has its parish and the Presbytery has its bounds so the Synod had its geographical area, its 'province', its full title being 'Provincial Synod'. There were twelve provinces, of comparable size acreage-wise but varying enormously population-wise – from Clydesdale (385 congregations and 209, 557 members) to Ross, Sutherland and Caithness (86 and 8642). To the twelve Scottish Synods had to be added the

Presbyteries of Orkney and of Shetland, each of which enjoyed full Synodical powers.

Its Members

The Synod consisted of all Ministers and Elders who were members of its constituent Presbyteries, and also a number of 'correspondents' – a Minister and an Elder from each of the contiguous Synods. This was a custom of ancient origin (1638) and as a gesture of interest and friendship is easily understood, but it is not clear why they should have been given a vote in matters which were no concern of theirs.

In 1981 legislation was introduced whereby a Synod might decide, given the concurrence of all its constituent Presbyteries, to confine its membership to an agreed proportion of its total strength, and some of the larger Synods availed themselves of the option – to no very obvious advantage.

Its Duties

The Synod had no power to legislate, but it could give orders. Under the Parliamentary Act of 1592 it had 'power to handle, order or redress all things omitted or done amiss' in the lower courts. It did not enjoy finality of judgment, however, the road to the Assembly being open to the dissatisfied litigant. In 1933 it was given finality in all cases other than those involving doctrine, worship, and the character of a Minister. This gave so much dissatisfaction in readjustment cases that in 1962 these were added to the list of exceptions.

In general terms it can be said that the Synod oversaw the work of the Presbyteries within its province.

The decision to abolish was no sudden affair. As far back as 1940 the Baillie Commission had advanced the suggestion that the Synod had served its day and generation, but in 1964 it was pointed out that constitutional difficulties stood in the way of its going. This was a reference to the fact that in the Articles Declaratory the Synod is declared to be part of the Presbyterian structure.

The arguments for abolition were two in particular. First, it was said that changes in the pattern of our government, particularly the emergence of the Assembly committee system, had rendered such an 'in-between' court no longer necessary. Quite simply the function of the Synod had been taken over.

And, second, the Synod had become impaled on the horns of a dilemma. If it were to be entrusted with a responsible job to do, it had to be better attended. But until it was given some measure of responsibility there was little likelihood of its attracting better attendance.

5
WHAT IS
THE GENERAL ASSEMBLY?

The General Assembly is the supreme ruling body within the Kirk, standing as it does at the peak of the pyramid of courts. Its decisions are final and binding on all within the fellowship of the Kirk; and in all matters that fall properly within its province. Its judgments are unassailable and cannot be made the subject of review in any civil court. The Assembly is really three courts rolled into one, and its functions can be divided into three categories – legislative, judicial, and administrative.

The Assembly meets in Edinburgh in a hall

on The Mound in the middle of May each year, convening on a Saturday and sitting each day through to the following Friday. Each Assembly is a separate and complete entity (unlike the Presbytery which adjourns from one meeting till the next), and so when the last item on the agenda has been overtaken the Moderator 'dissolves' the Assembly, an Act having already been passed appointing when and where the next Assembly is 'to be holden'.

Some of the most important Assemblies of the past have been held elsewhere than in Edinburgh – those in Perth and Glasgow spring readily to mind – but it is more convenient today to hold the Assembly in the capital city, and there it is likely to continue. There were troublous years for the Kirk in the seventeenth century when sometimes an Assembly did not meet, or its doings were later declared irregular, or it was dispersed by English troops; but from 1694 onwards an Assembly has met each year without exception, and this too is likely to be the ongoing pattern – though one occasionally hears talk of biennial Assemblies.

For long the Assembly was made up of Ministers and Elders from the Presbyteries, Universities, and Royal Burghs, but for some time past it has been only Presbyteries that have appointed Commissioners, Ministers and Elders, one of each for every four Ministers in the Presbytery, and lately members of the Diaconate. The choice of Elders is not restricted to members of Presbytery, any *bona fide* Elder being eligible. In practice most Presbyteries work on a rota whereby every fourth year opportunity is given to each Minister to attend and to each Kirk Session to nominate an Elder for election. You will sometimes hear it said that it is a particular Session's 'turn' to be 'represented', or that this is the year when the Rev So-and-so 'has the right to attend'. Both statements are quite misleading.

It is the Presbytery which has the right to be represented, and it has the right also to choose whom it will to represent it. There is also in recent days a small group of officials (eight in all) who attend *ex officiis.*

It is interesting and illuminating to note the terms of the commission. Those appointed are instructed 'to repair thereto, and to attend all the diets of the same, and there to consult and determine in all matters that come before them to the glory of God and the good of His Church, according to the Word of God, the Confession of Faith, and agreeable to the constitution of this Church, as they will be answerable'. That is to say, they are commissioners not delegates; they cannot be instructed how they are to cast their votes in any issue expected to arise.

Law-making Body

The General Assembly deliberates on all matters connected with the doctrine, government and discipline of the Church, and may pass Acts which thereby become standards for the Church. If all that is being done is formally to declare what is accepted as the law and practice of the Kirk, the Assembly can immediately pass a Declaratory Act. If, on the other hand, what is envisaged is some major change that is to become a binding rule and constitution for the Church then the proposed change must first be formulated as an Overture and sent down to Presbyteries which have to vote simply Approve or Disapprove. Only when more than half of the Presbyteries of the Church have indicated approval may the following Assembly pass an Act – though even then it is not bound to do so.

If the proposed new legislation is such as to involve any modification of, or addition to, the Declaratory Articles, this would have to go down to Presbyteries in two successive years and receive the assent of two-thirds of them on each occasion. Only then could the succeeding Assembly pass an Act to give it the force of law. This was recently exemplified in the dissolution of Synods (*qv*).

Court of Justice

The General Assembly is the supreme court of appeal. In litigation involving any matter of importance it is competent to persist from the Kirk Session through the Presbytery right to the General Assembly.

It is doubtful whether a body the size and constitution of the Assembly is suited for the dispensing of justice in delicate issues. Attempts have been made to improve the machinery in such cases. Where the character and conduct of a Minister are involved there now exists a Judicial Commission charged with the duty of hearing the evidence and reaching a finding thereanent. It was felt necessary, though, to leave the Assembly itself to ratify the verdict and pass sentence. The weakness of this, obviously, is that to determine a fair sentence it is necessary to know more about the affair than hearing the charge and learning that the verdict was 'Guilty'. Questions are asked from the floor and almost inescapably a retrial is being held – which is utterly unsatisfactory. It is difficult to see how even an all-powerful Assembly can at one and the same time delegate its power and retain the right to say the last word.

Organ of Administration

Most of the time of a present-day Assembly is occupied with matters of administration. Standing Committees submit reports of their diligence during the past year and seek approval of policies for the future. When we remember that the book of Assembly reports can run to about 600 closely printed pages we get some impression of the amount of administration involved, and when we compare this with the modest print of cases which covers both legislative and judicial aspects of the Assembly we see how completely the supreme court of the Kirk is coming to be primarily an organ of administration.

A Rip-van-Winkle commissioner awakening in today's Assembly would be much mystified by all this. He would have no need to be worried, though, for a living Kirk must be able to accommodate itself to changing situations. And if today sees more administration and less litigation, who is to say this is necessarily a bad thing – even if it makes for a much duller Assembly.

6
WHAT IS
A MODERATOR?

EVERY court of the Church of Scotland has a Moderator. His position is comparable to that of a Chairman in that, occupying the chair, it is for him 'to announce matters, to cause good order to be kept, and to ascertain the vote'; but he is more than a Chairman in that he is responsible for calling, or declining to call, meetings, and he differs from the normal Chairman in that he has no deliberative but only a casting vote. It is worth noting that a decision of the Court of Session in 1830 has established that unless there is statute law or inveterate custom to the contrary, a Chairman has only a deliberative vote.

Beyond the power to keep good order in his court, the Moderator enjoys no kind or degree of authority. On a point of order, his is the last word, though of course he is answerable to the superior courts. On a point of order a Moderator may if so minded ask the court to vote, but even then it is he who must accept responsibility and rule. Once he has given a decision that becomes a judgment of the court and can be made the subject of appeal just like any other.

In the Kirk Session

The *Form of Presbyterian Church Government* (1645) states that 'it is most expedient that the Moderator of Kirk Session should be a minister'. This has always been our accepted practice and is now held to be settled law. Normally it is the Minister of the Parish who is Moderator of its Session. During a vacancy or when the Minister has been granted leave of absence, the Presbytery appoints another Minister as Moderator *ad interim*. In an emergency and under very strict safeguards, any other Minister may be authorised by the regular Moderator to act at a specified meeting to carry through specific business, as Moderator *pro tempore*.

The identification of the Minister of the Parish with the Moderator of its Kirk Session can lead to confusion. In an item of business affecting the parish the Minister can have two distinct – and even conflicting – interests, as Moderator of Session and as Parish Minister. Hence it is important that a petition, for example, should be signed twice by the Moderator – as Parish Minister and as Moderator of Session.

A tendency is prevalent to address the chair as Moderator at, for example, a meeting of Deacons' Court or of Congregational Board, the proper designation being 'Mr Chairman'. It should be said too that there is no justification for 'Mr Moderator' – he (or she) is simply 'Moderator'.

In Presbytery

Presbyteries choose their own Moderator; they do so by free election from among the Ministers, and he or she holds office for at least a year, being eligible for re-election. In 1996 an Act was passed extending the choice to include Elders and

Deacons, but, so far as I know, no Presbytery has taken advantage of this. One can understand this, for such a Moderator would not be able to lay-on hands at an ordination. It has to be said, though, that in 1600 in the Presbytery of Glasgow a vote was taken between two aspirants, the successful one being a schoolmaster.

The so-called *Bishops Report* which was before the Assembly in 1957 advanced the proposition that 'a permanent Bishop-in-Presbytery would take the place of the changing Moderator'. Such bishops were to be 'chosen by each Presbytery, from its own membership or otherwise'. Later ecumenical reports have suggested either permanency or a fairly long period in office. Both proposals spring from a complete misapprehension of the character of the Presbytery and of the position of its Moderator. All Ministers of the Presbytery are equal in status; any one of them may be chosen to act as Moderator for a year; he is vested with authority to rule, but only in the conduct of meetings and only if these are in session. The temporary character of the Moderatorship is neither incidental nor accidental, it reflects our conception of the nature of the office.

In the General Assembly

Strictly and traditionally all that has been said about the Moderator of Presbytery applies equally to the Moderator of the General Assembly, but of late there has been a process steadily gaining momentum designed to turn the Moderator into a leading figure within the Kirk, frequently referred to quite inaccurately as 'Moderator of the Church of Scotland'.

It is for the Assembly to choose its own Moderator, and in so doing it is no longer confined to Ministers. Until the Assembly meets and is constituted, it is not known who are commissioners from among whom the choice falls to be made. The proper course would be, then, that once the Assembly was constituted we should look around and ask, 'Whom will we have for our Moderator?' Obviously when so much has to be done by the person chosen – at the Assembly itself, during the following months when he has to arrange for a year's absence from his ordinary duties, when so much preparation has to be done – obviously such 'instant choice' would be utterly impracticable. Nowadays the Moderator is nominated at a meeting in October of a special committee, and for some years now he has become *ex officio* a member of Assembly. He has still to be elected by the Assembly, but this, of necessity, is now a sheer formality.

On a strict interpretation the authority of the Moderator holds only so long as his court is in session and once he has solemnly dissolved that court on the closing day he automatically resumes his former status. Early in the century it was felt there were areas in the extreme west and north of the country much cut off from the main stream of Church life and that it would be a great encouragement and strength to them were they to have a visit from the Moderator conveying the greetings of the Church.

From this innocent beginning the custom developed whereby the Moderator is expected in the months between Assemblies – his 'year of office' – to visit five or six Presbyteries for about ten days each, to visit Scottish Forces units in Europe and farther afield, to visit Presbyterian Churches in many parts of the world, to visit Churches in Africa and India with which the Kirk has close relations, to attend national occasions in London – and so on. It is an exhausting, if exhilarating and richly rewarding, experience.

There are those who would like to see the Moderator of Assembly given authority in name of the Church in the period between Assemblies,

but this has been consistently and strenuously –
and rightly – resisted.

7
WHAT, OR WHO,
IS COX?

'ACCORDING to Cocker' is a phrase commonly
used to mean spot-on-correct, beyond all possible
challenge. Edward Cocker was a mathematician
of the seventeenth century whose book on Arith-
metic ran to 16 editions. His was the last word of
authority. The corresponding phrase in the Kirk is
'according to Cox'.

Revd James Taylor Cox was Minister at Dyce
and Principal Clerk of Assembly both before and
after the Union of 1929. In 1934 he published a
book on Church Law which is now in its sixth
edition and which is still accepted as the last
word on any question of procedure within the
Kirk. If you are all right according to Cox you
have nothing to fear, your position is secure.

When today we speak of 'Cox' we are referring to the book *Practice and Procedure in the Church
of Scotland,* first published in September 1934
under the editorship of Dr Cox and later revised
by him. Still later (1964) the work was revised
and updated by Dr James B Longmuir, and then
in 1976 by Revd D F M Macdonald. It is now
out-of-print and almost impossible to procure.

Some ten years ago it was agreed that the
time for 'editions' was past and serious thought
was given to the possibility of producing a
completely new work, the project being put in
hand. Delays have occurred but this has now
made its appearance from the pen of Dr James
Weatherhead under the title *The Constitution and
Laws of the Church of Scotland* and is to be read
alongside of the *Book of Acts of the General Assembly*
– a work, obviously, to which additions have to

be made as each successive Assembly passes new legislation.

Sources of 'Cox'

It is early yet to say how future generations will say 'according to ....', but it is interesting to discover where 'Cox' came from. An eminent professor of Scots Law has it on record that the secret of writing any text-book on law is discreet plagiarising. I am sure this is true. Here you have a sphere which allows no room for originality (except in presentation), or for imagination (except for seeing the pitfalls open to the unwary), and most certainly not for poetic language (for that can be dangerously misleading). The whole thing is already determined and decided to the last detail – all that is needed is to write it down clearly and distinctly – a daunting enough undertaking in all conscience.

It is no criticism of Dr Cox to say that much of what we find in his book is already set forth either in *Digest of Church Laws* by William Mair (first published in 1887), the standard work in the Church of Scotland (and of the fourth edition of which he, Dr Cox, had been editor), or in *Manual of Practice and Procedure in the United Free Church of Scotland*, the corresponding work from the other side. The latter book in turn was compiled after the Union of 1900 to combine the wisdom of *Practice of the Free Church of Scotland* and *Rules and Forms Procedure in the United Presbyterian Church*. Mair's work in turn was preceded by another dating from 1838, *Styles of Writ, Forms of Procedure, and Practice of the Church Courts of Scotland,* edited by Dr Cook of Haddington – though this was more a collection of styles than a text-book.

To all that was in these earlier books, Cox added a vast amount concerning the new law that had inevitably followed upon the Union as well as what was contained in the Basis of Union itself.

This was largely of a declaratory character clarifying where the united Church stood in matters where there had been diversity of practice – of vital importance to the new Church at that stage.

Statutory Enactment

It is interesting to note that not one of these law books mentioned, with the exception of Mair, so much as uses 'law' in its title, and in particular that Dr Cox should have claimed no more for his work than that it represented the practice and procedure of the Kirk. The reason for this insistence on practice in preference to law is that the law of the Church of Scotland is far from being a simple affair of Assembly legislation, a collection of statutes capable of easy codification. The rules governing the Kirk derive from a variety of sources: Acts of Parliament, Acts of Assembly, long-established custom, decided cases.

It is more in connection with the constitution of the Church than with the management of its day-to-day affairs that we have to turn to Acts of Parliament for our authority. Obviously a Church which is 'established by law' should be able to find statutory authority for its constitution, and there are a number of Acts which are of considerable importance of this character.

Of much greater importance for ordinary purposes are the Acts of Assembly, and these may be said today to constitute the principal source of Church law. Any such enactments which are to become 'binding rules and constitutions for the Church' cannot at once be enacted by any one Assembly but must be sent down to Presbyteries under the Barrier Act, thus investing the lower court with what amounts to a power of veto. As recent examples of this type of legislation one thinks of the creation of the Auxiliary Ministry, changing the rules for filling vacancies, amending the character of the Judicial Commission.

It should be added that once a matter has been dealt with in this way, the Act becomes the final authority to the exclusion of all other. If, for example, the Act anent Membership of Presbytery says that no Minister may have a seat in Presbytery except in terms of this Act, then it is useless to plead that there has been a long-established practice of securing a seat in some other fashion.

Precedent and Custom

As is the case with our civil law, so our ecclesiastical law depends upon decided cases. The principle of *stare decisis* is not in the General Assembly an absolute and binding rule, but it will be followed unless for some compelling reason. After all, if a court is to hold the confidence of the people as supreme judiciary it must be seen to be consistent. Law in so many cases has its root in custom. In the law of the Kirk – as of the land – long-established practice will constitute law. An obvious example has to do with the admission of women to the ministry. When it was decided to make this change there was no written law to be amended. Search the law-books in vain to find it written down that a woman could not be a Minister. It was the law of the Kirk none the less and it required an Act with the support of the Presbyteries before things could be otherwise.

The law of the Kirk is something that has been built up over the centuries as the result sometimes of almost instinctive action, sometimes of deliberative decision; it has been summarised in its main outlines in Cox (and Weatherhead).

I deliberately refrain from making reference to my own production *The Law and Practice of the Kirk* (1996) for this was never intended to be a manual of law comparable in any way with Cox, but rather a fairly simple hand-book for the guidance of office-bearers and others.

HISTORIC DOCUMENTS

THE problem in regard to Historic Documents lies in knowing which to select – there have been so many which, over the centuries, have each in its own particular way played a part in determining the shape of today's Kirk. Therefore choice has been restricted to seven of what may be seen as having been crucial in making the Church of Scotland what it is today: the two Books of Discipline – Knox's and Melville's – which laid the sure foundation of its Presbyterian constitution; the two Covenants (1638 and 1643) – which between them played so large a part in the final defeat of the attempt to foist Episcopacy upon an unwilling Kirk, and then in later years kept re-emerging as bones of contention within denominations; the Westminster Confession, the work that has provided a creed for successive generations and for which we have not yet been able to find a successor; the Revolution Settlement, in some ways more an event than a document, but playing an important role in establishing for all time the Presbyterian form of Church government as agreeable to the Word of God; and then finally the Articles Declaratory, the document which sets forth in the most unequivocal terms the Kirk's claim to autonomy and the State's acceptance of and support for that claim, with all that that implies.

8

WHAT ARE THE BOOKS OF DISCIPLINE?

FROM the earliest days of the Reformation it has been maintained that one of the marks of a true Kirk is that 'discipline is richtly entertaynlt' – translated in the Articles Declaratory as 'Discipline rightly exercised'. Understandably one is inclined to equate discipline with the moral inquisition exercised by the eighteenth century Kirk Session with its stool of repentance and its pulpit rebuke. That was, of course, one aspect of discipline, but the word had a much wider connotation and referred to the whole business of Church government. A Book of Discipline was essentially a constitution.

There have in the Church of Scotland been two such books. The First Book of Discipline, with which the name of John Knox is popularly associated, was produced in May 1560, the Second being accepted by the Church 21 years later. It bore the name of Andrew Melville and officially superseded the earlier work.

First Book of Discipline

The official date of the Scottish Reformation is 24th August 1560, that being the day when the Scottish Parliament sanctioned a new creed or confession of faith, abolished papal jurisdiction, repealed earlier legislation in favour of the Roman Church, and abolished the mass, ordaining penalties for hearers and sayers of the same. Some four months before this, on 29th April, five distinguished Scottish Churchmen were commissioned to prepare a Book of Discipline. They were Knox, Spottiswood, Winram, Willock, and Ross, and by an odd coincidence each bore the Christian name of John. This was the same body which, with the addition of John Douglas, had in four days produced the Scots Confession. They did not waste time over their second task either, for on 29th May the completed document was ready. It was accepted by the General Assembly and it has appended to it no fewer than 33 of Scotland's most famous names. But it was never to receive Parliamentary approval, doubtless because it demanded for its implementation more money than Parliament was prepared to make available. There is a familiar ring about the criticism of proposals that look like costing too much – that they are 'devout imaginings'.

In a document running to 56 pages the authors enter into a lot of needless detail. Had they taken a little more time editing back the work they may have considerably enhanced its value. It set itself to face the practical problems confronting the new Church, and that in a most down-to-earth fashion. There were to be five offices within the Kirk – Minister, Reader, Superintendent, Elder and Deacon. Every congregation was to have the right to call its own Minister, though failure to do so within forty days gave Church the right to step in and make an appointment. In line with the Reformers' bitter hatred of anything smacking remotely of idolatry, ordination by the laying-on of hands was deliberately rejected because, they argued, 'albeit the apostles used the imposition of hands, yet, seeing the miracle is ceased, the using of the ceremonie we judge not necessarie'.

Ministers were in short supply. Not by any means all of the Roman Priests had come over, and new Ministers, if they were to be properly trained, took time to prepare, so there was an interim shortage. To meet this there was created the office of Reader, a kind of substitute Minister who did not baptise, marry, or celebrate Communion, but who conducted the ordinary service (there was a prayer book), and who, while supposed not to preach, was permitted after reading the Scripture to add a few words by way of explanation. Between 1567 and 1574 the number of Readers increased from 415 to 715 while the Ministers remained fairly constant in the 250-300 range. In 1581 the Assembly agreed to abolish the office of Reader, but in the remote areas they continued to function long after that.

The office of Superintendent – there were to be ten – is one of no little interest, bearing as it does an uncanny resemblance to that of Bishop, the area assigned to each being even referred to as a diocese. Their job was the planting of kirks and the provision of Ministers and Readers. They were to be constantly on the move, not more than twenty days in any one place or up to four months in their principal station. This office, like that of Reader, was looked upon as a temporary expedient that would obtain only until all necessary kirks had been planted and filled.

'Men of best knowledge of God's Word and cleanest life' were to be elected Elders and Deacons and their duties would be to superintend the behaviour of the people, and the care of the poor. They were to be subject to yearly election lest by long continuance in office they should presume to encroach upon the liberty of the Church.

Second Book of Discipline

A completely new chapter of constitutional Church history for Scotland was begun with the appearance of Andrew Melville. A brilliant scholar, able organiser and dedicated Presbyterian, he was to set the stamp of his personal genius upon Scottish Presbyterian polity. A man who knew his own mind, he was afraid of none.

Melville's hostility to episcopacy took shape in the Second Book of Discipline, which was adopted by the Church in 1581. The number of offices was reduced to four – Minister (bishop or pastor), Doctor (teacher), Elder (presbyter), and Deacon. Ministers were to be ordained by the laying-on of hands – 'ordination is the separation and sanctifying of the person appointed by God and His Kirk after he be well tried and found qualified'. Elders (still to be elected annually) were to assist the Minister in the spiritual supervision of the parish, watching over the moral behaviour of the people. Deacons would continue to be the body responsible for the care of the poor.

The government of the Church was to be the business of a hierarchy of courts, and it was here that for the first time Presbyteries appeared. The civil magistrate was to assist and maintain the Church, to make sure that it was able to make its judgments effective, and 'to maintain the liberty and quietness of the Kirk'.

The Second Book of Discipline received Parliamentary sanction in an Act of 1592, of which the historian Cook has this to say:

> *It placed the ministers in the situation which they had long been desirous to occupy; it gave them reason to hope that, secured against opposition they might devote themselves to the spiritual concerns of the community, and it afforded to the King an opportunity of gaining their confidence and, through this, the best wishes and steady loyalty of his people.*

9
WHAT WERE THE COVENANTS?

THERE were two Covenants: the National Covenant of 1638 and the Solemn League and Covenant of 1643. They were as different as could be in both intent and content.

The idea of binding together in a covenant obviously had its roots in Scripture and it clearly was a concept that much commended itself to the Scots. Let us then look with some care at these two documents, for between them they do much to explain great tracts of Scottish history.

It is hard to say when events first began to build up into the situation from which the National Covenant sprang, but let us start with the year 1626 which saw the accession of King Charles I to the joint throne. Without doubt Charles was a better man than his father James I, but he was lacking in that craftiness that had so often come to the rescue of his father. He had, however, inherited the paternal determination to be an absolute monarch and with this in view to bring the Scots Kirk into line with her southern neighbour. Two formidable obstacles stood in his way: an English Parliament resolved to extend democratic rights and a Scots Kirk dedicated to maintain the Crown Rights of Christ.

Charles had the remarkably sound idea that if the two peoples could be brought to adopt the same pattern of worship they would be a long way on the road towards religious unification. So the preparation of a Book of Common Prayer was put in hand. All might have gone well, but by way of preparation the monarch decided to issue a Book of Canons with an order that this be observed by all clergy. In all the circumstances it was a remarkably silly document – for example one of the canons made it an offence worthy of excommunication to say that the Book of Common Prayer contained anything repugnant to Scripture, the said book being still in course of preparation. Scottish hackles were instantly raised. A perfectly reasoned petition was presented to the Privy Council. In more violent – and more immediately telling fashion – the herb-stall woman Jenny Geddes hurled her stool at the head of the celebrant in St Giles' shouting, 'Villain, durst thou say mass in my lug'.

The National Covenant

So it was that early in 1638 the supporters of the freedom of the Kirk gathered in Edinburgh to put their names to the National Covenant. This was a document prepared by a Minister and a Lawyer and, considering the provocation to which the Kirk had been subjected, a remarkably subdued and reasonable affair.

It was in three parts. First it repeated what was generally known as the Negative Confession, drawn up in 1580, signed by the King himself, consisting of an uncompromising rejection of Rome and all her works. Second, it listed all the many Acts which the Scots Parliament had passed against Romanism. Third was a short section, a declaration of intent, the determination of the signatories 'to recover the purity and liberty of the Gospel', with a prayer 'that religion and righteousness may flourish in the land to the glory

THE NATIONAL COVENANT, SIGNED IN GREYFRIARS GRAVEYARD

of God, the honour of our King, and the peace and comfort of all'. This was not revolutionary or treasonable – not on the face of it; though maybe Charles showed more understanding than normal when he said that so long as the Covenant was in force his authority in Scotland was practically nothing – adding the prophetic words, 'a position I would rather die than accept'.

The Glasgow Assembly

The National Covenant proved an instant and overwhelming success. Signing began in Greyfriars graveyard on 28th February 1638 amid scenes of great excitement. People of all classes and conditions flocked to add their names, it being said that when ink ran out they signed in their own blood, a portent, surely, of things to come. Copies appeared all round the country to be subscribed with like enthusiasm.

ON 28TH FEBRUARY 1638 AMID SCENES OF GREAT EXCITEMENT.

35

Scarcely ever has Scotland seen such unanimity.

The King took fright. It was time the Scots were taught a lesson. But that meant an army which in turn meant money, and money meant taxation, which meant recalling Parliament. And all of it meant time. So by way of temporising he agreed that an Assembly should meet at Glasgow in November. It would be the first Assembly for twenty years, the first free Assembly for thirty years, so it is not surprising that it took its head. At the end of a week the King's Commissioner, having been unable to hold it in rein, solemnly dissolved it in name of the Sovereign and departed. However it sat on for the next three weeks and, as can so easily happen, not content with repealing the tyrannical legislation of the past years it contributed its own share of tyrannical legislation against others. Sad indeed that within a matter of months a great document of freedom should have become an instrument of oppression.

The Solemn League and Covenant

Clearly the King was not going to accept this with equanimity, so a strong Covenanting army was got together under the able General Leslie with for its banner 'Christ's Crown and Covenant'. Charles took the field, but finding himself confronting a much superior force he temporised again, promising to accept in matters spiritual the judgments of the Assembly, and in matters civil those of the Scots Parliament. By the late summer of 1640 Charles had contrived to muster an army, financed by loans from wealthy Londoners and this marched north to Newcastle where it was swept aside by the Covenanters who, occupying Newcastle and Durham, sent a deputation south to negotiate with the Sovereign.

It is historical fact that victims of oppression, once in control, can be awful tyrants. Unhappily the word 'Covenant' became equated with 'oppression', seen in two forms – first in a Puritanism quite foreign to Scotland but strongly present in the English Parliament; and second in the Solemn League and Covenant signed in Edinburgh in 1643 by the Presbyterian leaders and by a deputation from the English Parliament. Its two aims: to make common cause against the throne and to make the Churches of the three kingdoms as like one another as possible, on Presbyterian lines.

The National Covenant was an attempt by Scots to resist having thrust upon them an alien form of worship they detested; the later Covenant was an alliance of Scots with a minority party in the South dedicated to imposing the Scots form of religion upon the whole of England and Ireland. From the outset it was doomed to failure.

The Solemn League and Covenant, however, was not all loss for the Scots. By an odd quirk of fate it was responsible for four things that have meant much for the life of our Kirk – the Westminster Confession, the two Catechisms, and the Metrical Psalms.

10

WHAT IS THE WESTMINSTER CONFESSION?

The Church of Scotland holds as its subordinate standard the Westminster Confession of Faith, recognising liberty of opinion on such points of doctrine as do not enter into the substance of the faith, and claiming the right, in dependence on the promised guidance of the Holy Spirit, to formulate, interpret, or modify its subordinate standards; always in agreement with the Word of God and the fundamental doctrines of the Christian faith contained in the said Confession – of which agreement the Church itself shall be sole judge.

THUS concludes the preamble read at all services of ordination or induction in the Kirk. In an earlier paragraph the Church had reaffirmed its acceptance of the Scriptures of the Old and New Testaments as the supreme rule of faith and life. Very shortly the Candidate is going to be asked, 'Do you believe the fundamental doctrines of the Christian faith contained in the Confession of Faith of this Church?'

The question 'What is the Westminster Confession?' is a very pertinent one indeed.

What is its History?

The most significant and lasting outcome of the Solemn League and Covenant was the Westminster Assembly. It was constituted by an ordnance of the Lords and Commons of England on 12th June 1643 'that such government may be settled in the Church as may be most agreeable to God's Holy Word, and most apt to procure and preserve the peace of the Church at home, and nearer agreement with the Church of Scotland and other Reformed Churches abroad'. Ten peers, twenty members of the Commons and 121 Ministers were appointed, but the day before they were due to meet the King declared the whole affair illegal and only 69 of the 121 were prepared to ignore the royal embargo. Commissioners from Scotland attended by invitation and made their voices heard. The complete absence of an Episcopal voice was unfortunate, for it meant the deliberations had a definite slant.

During its five years' existence the Assembly got through a lot of business producing, as well as the Confession, the Larger and the Shorter Catechisms, the Directory for the Public Worship of God, the Form of Presbyterian Church Government, and a new version of the Metrical Psalms. All bear a tang of Puritanism, but the Puritan influence in Scotland then was not inconsiderable.

The Westminster Confession of Faith 1647 deals with the Churches' beliefs. Calvinistic in outlook, it lays great stress on Scripture. It speaks of God, the Trinity, Predestination and Election, the Fall of Man, Justification, Saving Faith, Repentance unto Life, the Civil Magistrate, the Church, the Sacraments. It is a long and detailed document that deals faithfully with many difficult theological problems. Inevitably as a product of its time it bears the scars of contemporary warfare, but it contrives to rise above that, grappling with the deepest thinking of all the ages on the eternal things of the faith.

During the period succeeding the Reformation, Scotland had known at least three Confessions. First there was 'Patrick's Places', the work of Patrick Hamilton, the martyr. This was a simple statement of evangelical truth, largely Lutheran in tone. Second there was the 'First Helvetic Confession', a statement emanating from the Evangelical Swiss Cantons, translated *circa* 1640 by George Wishart. Then there was also the 'Scots Confession' of 1560, which John Knox and the other five Johns cobbled together in four days when Parliament wanted a statement of the Reformed Faith and which struck a distinctly Calvinistic note. It is odd, and perhaps unfortunate, that the Scottish Kirk should have allowed these documents, so closely associated with her own Reformation, to be largely forgotten while clinging tenaciously to a document produced in England by Englishmen at the behest of an English Parliament!

What is its Status?

As we all know, it is the subordinate standard of the Church, but what is a subordinate standard — and why should it be 'the' rather than 'a'? The answer to the former question is that for the Scottish Churchman nothing can challenge the position of Scripture – every standard must take its place somewhere behind the Bible. Let Confession and Scripture be at variance, it is the former that must go. The authors of the Scots Confession made this very clear in their Preface:

> *We conjure you if any man will note in this our Confession any article or sentence repugnant to God's Holy Word, that it would please him of his gentleness, and for Christian charity's sake to admonish us the same in writing, and we, upon our honour and fidelity, do promise him satisfaction from Holy Scriptures or due reformation of that which he shall prove to be amiss.*

And to the latter question. In signalling it as the subordinate standard the Church is saying simply that this is the confession to which its officers must subscribe. Other confessions there may be, interesting and historic documents, but this holds a special place shared with no other.

It is not an absolute standard for it is hedged about with a conscience clause – it recognises liberty of opinion on such points of doctrine as do not enter into the substance of the faith, though this does not confer a freedom to accept or reject at will, for it applies only to those matters that are not of the substance of the faith and it is for the Kirk herself to be Sole Judge of what these are. Some years ago the Assembly received a report on 'The Christian Use of Sunday' recommending a measure of freedom in this field utterly at variance with the position of the Confession. When in the end the recommendations were approved the Assembly, in my view declared that these things did not enter into the substance of the faith and accordingly the conscience clause could be invoked.

For a considerable time past the Confession has been consistently under attack from the side of those who feel that with the passing of the years it has lost much of its relevance so that it has little to say to the present generation – in short that we are in need of a new up-to-date model. At the opposite extreme there are those who see in the Confession something infinitely precious, linking us not only with all that is best and most to be treasured in our own past, but also with Presbyterians throughout the world. Somewhere between the two poles, probably, are to be found the majority of ordinary Kirk folk. The Confession may today leave a lot to be desired, but we must hold on to it until something better has been produced – and efforts so far have lamentably failed. This is the age of the explorer not of the cartographer – his day will come.

The Westminster Confession is today, if you will, very much an historic document, but as a distinguished Churchman once remarked in my hearing, 'The old battleship may bear the scars of many wars and be a bit dated, but we daren't scuttle her to set sail in a coracle'. That at least was the judgment of the Assembly of 1974.

11

WHAT WAS THE REVOLUTION SETTLEMENT?

WHEN in 1688 James II fled the country, the parishes of Scotland were all filled with Episcopal clergy, the Presbyterians having been hiding in moorland fastnesses for the past 28 years. The Dutch fleet, which had been bringing William of Orange to these shores, was driven back by adverse weather. The Scottish Bishops, seeing this as a providential intervention, sent a messenger to

James assuring him of their unshaken loyalty and hoping that his foot might soon be back on the neck of his enemies. When, however, William actually landed in England, the clergy became no less alarmed for the future of their Church than for their personal safety – not without cause as the event was to show.

In the south-west particularly, where the persecution had been at its most bitter, the revenge was most swift. By and large the curates had been men of poor quality and unpopular with their flocks against whom in many instances they had acted as informers, and it was not surprising, therefore, that the people did not wait for the passing of legislation to get rid of them. There immediately began a process known as the 'rabbling of the curates' whereby a mob attacked the manse, threw out (sometimes setting alight) the furniture, led the incumbent to the outskirts of the parish and with much indignity bade him farewell. Meantime the outed Ministers returned to their manses and resumed the work of their parishes. It was all very reprehensible – if very understandable. It is remarkable that although there were a couple of hundred rabblings in the south-west, the whole exercise was accomplished without the shedding of a drop of blood.

The issue developed in a more legal and regular fashion when in April 1689 in the Claim of Rights (in virtue of which the throne was offered to William and Mary) it was stipulated that Episcopacy should be abolished because 'prelacy and the superiority of any office in the Church above Presbyters is, and hath been, a great and insupportable grievance to this nation, and contrary to the inclinations of the generality of the people ever since the Reformation (they being reformed from Popery by Presbyters)'. Surprising is it not that they founded on a democratic note rather than with a reference to the Word of God.

The Kirk was indeed fortunate in that the new King's principal adviser in respect of Scottish affairs was William Carstares. Born in the Manse of Cathcart, where his father ministered before his translation to Glasgow's Outer High Kirk, Carstares was educated at the Universities of Edinburgh and Utrecht, being ordained to the ministry in Holland (like so many Presbyterians from Scotland at that time). His father was 'outed' from the High Kirk, and William himself, suspected of having been implicated in the Ryehouse plot, was brought to Scotland and subjected to the thumbscrews.

This understandably increased his standing in the eyes of the King when he returned to Holland to officiate at the Scots Church, Leyden. On coming to England the King brought Carstares with him, assigned him apartments in the Palace of Kensington, and made him his private chaplain. There is no doubt that Carstares' intimate knowledge of Scottish affairs, plus his own deep-set Presbyterianism, played a large part in shaping the new King's policy towards his northern kingdom.

The new monarch's natural inclination was all towards a policy of toleration. He was, too, accustomed in Holland to a form of Church government similar to the Presbyterian. His wife, on the other hand, had all the strong Episcopal leanings that brought her family so much trouble. Besides, from an administrative point of view it would have meant one form of religion obtaining north and south of the border. There was, however, one overriding consideration which a ruler in his precarious position dare not ignore. And that was the security of his own position on the throne – the Jacobites were never very far away.

The Convention of Estates was due to meet at this time, and in this the astute William saw the opportunity for having his purposes achieved without seeming himself to have acted in an arbitrary fashion. But there were difficulties. Under the law as it stood no one could sit on the Convention until he had taken oath abduring the Covenants and accepting the doctrine of the King's supremacy in all matters ecclesiastical. In such circumstances the Convention could do no other than support Episcopacy. The King had the courage to dispense with the oath and to ordain that the burgh representatives were to be appointed on a poll of the inhabitants. The Estates met at Edinburgh on 14th February 1689 with a momentous agenda – they had to decide who was to reign in Scotland and they had to settle what would be the religion of the nation. Right away it became apparent that the Orange party was in the ascendancy when by a majority of forty the Duke of Hamilton was elected President in preference to the Duke of Atholl.

The Convention declared that James VII was a Papist who had violated the laws and had thereby forfeited his throne, and they went on to resolve that William and Mary should be declared King and Queen of Scotland – a resolution opposed by only nine – of whom seven were Bishops.

They further went on to declare their determination in regard to the Church – a position later ratified by the King who agreed to establish by law that form of Church government in this kingdom which is 'most agreeable to the inclinations of the people'. Thus was Episcopacy set aside and the Presbyterianism of 1592 revived, the outed ministers restored, the Westminster Confession confirmed, and the first General Assembly since 1653 summoned for 3rd October 1690. It is worth noting that there was no claim that Presbyterianism was of divine appointment, or that it was superior to episcopacy – only that it was what the people wanted.

Next, Episcopacy as ratified by law was formally abolished, and the Act of Supremacy by which Charles had set himself up as dictator in all matters ecclesiastical was duly annulled.

Third patronage was abolished. King William was not happy about this (you could have too much democracy), but he was prepared to concede the point, moved to no small extent doubtless by the realisation that the continuance of patronage would lead to parishes being filled by Jacobite sympathisers. That is another story to be told in another place.

The Revolution Settlement was a great triumph for Presbyterianism in Scotland.

12
WHAT ARE THE
ARTICLES DECLARATORY?

THE Union in 1929 of the United Free Church of Scotland with the ongoing Church of Scotland was achieved only after many years of patient and painstaking negotiation. One of the main obstacles to the flowing together of these two main streams of Christian witness in Scotland lay in the relationship believed to exist on the parish side between Church and State. The UF Church was intensely dedicated to everything represented by the word 'Free' while her opposite number was no less proud of being 'Established'. As so often happens, no small part of the difficulty sprang not from the actual principles but from mistaken ideas popularly held in regard to what these principles meant.

With a view to demythologising the idea of establishment the leaders on the Church of Scotland side conceived the idea of setting forth and having ratified by an Act of Parliament what was the position of the Kirk *vis-à-vis* the State. Thus there emerged the Church of Scotland Act 1921 with its schedule headed 'Articles Declaratory of the Constitution of the Church of Scotland in Matters Spiritual'. The material had in 1919 been approved by a very large majority of Presbyteries, had subsequently been approved by both Houses of Parliament, and had received the Royal Assent on 28th July 1921. Their becoming effective was once more delayed until they had again obtained Presbytery approval and until another Bill affecting property and endowments had become an Act, so that it was not until 28th June 1926 that an Order in Council made the Act operative.

Declaratory

The first thing to be noted about the Act is that it is declaratory: it does not make law, it merely states what the law is. The Kirk was insistent on this. It was not a case where Parliament was conferring freedom, power, autonomy on a Church devoid of these, all parliament was doing was recognising a *de facto* situation established through years of struggle and sacrifice. The authority for the freedom of the Kirk is to be found not in the statute books but in the history books.

The first of the Articles constitutes a remarkably clear and succinct statement of the doctrinal position of the Kirk – so much so that suggestions have from time to time been advanced that its terms might be accepted as a statement of the fundamental doctrines of the Church to which, insofar as they enter into the substance of the faith, Ministers and Office-bearers are committed. The position of the first Article is unique in that it is the one which not even the Church itself has power to modify or add to, since, as interpreted by the Church, it is essential to its continuity and corporate life. So far as doctrine is concerned, what we have is an identikit portrait of the Kirk. This does not mean we can never change; but if we do change we will no longer be what we are now – though that seems rather obvious!

Article II accepts the Westminster Confession as principal subordinate standard, declares the government of the Church to be Presbyterian, and sets forth the standards that govern its system, principles of worship, orders, and discipline.

The third Article claims for the Kirk historical continuity with the Scottish Church reformed in 1560, whose liberties were ratified in 1592 and whose security was guaranteed in the Treaty of Union of 1707. Having thus proclaimed the rights of the Kirk, the Article goes on to affirm its acceptance of its 'distinctive call and duty to bring the ordinances of religion to the people in every parish of Scotland through a territorial ministry'.

Reference has already been made to the declaration of independence contained in Article IV. It begins with a claim to belong to the Universal Church and to receive from Christ its Divine King and Head and from Him alone power, subject to the civil authority, to legislate and to adjudicate finally in all matters of doctrine, worship, government and discipline.

The following Article (V) claims the inherent right (once again and very emphatically 'free from interference by civil authority') to 'frame or adopt its subordinate standards, to declare the sense in which it understands its Confession of Faith, to modify the forms of expression therein, or to formulate other doctrinal statements'; and it concludes with a claim that in any question arising in regard to its exercise of these powers it itself is to be 'sole Judge'.

Article VI is the really tricky one. It begins by accepting the divine appointment and authority of the civil magistrate within his own sphere, and goes on to declare that Church and State owe mutual duties one to the other. But then it makes the amazing claim that 'the Church and State have the right to determine each for itself all questions concerning the extent and continuance of their mutual relations in the discharge of their duties and the obligations arising therefrom'. If two parties are at loggerheads on a question in which each has a material interest, how can each be entitled unilaterally to determine the rights and wrongs of the question – let alone the practical action to be taken in relation to it? What the Article seems to say is, 'We're not going to dictate to you, but you, certainly, will not dictate to us'. This, it is respectfully submitted, is to create, not to solve, a problem.

Article VII is often quoted in course of the ecumenical debate, for it puts the Church under obligation to seek and to prosecute union with other Churches. But it leaves to the Church to satisfy itself that these are Churches where the Word is purely preached, the Sacraments administered according to Christ's ordinance and discipline rightly administered. You could scarcely ask for more freedom than that.

The penultimate Article sets up the machinery whereby any of the provisions (except Article I) may be 'modified or added to' given a two-thirds majority of Presbyteries on being sent down in two successive years. The ninth and final Article ratifies and confirms the foregoing as the Constitution of the Church of Scotland in Matters Spiritual.

It is quite a document.

CHURCH
AND
STATE

IT seems to be universally agreed that in Scotland over the centuries we have contrived to work out a sound relationship between Church and State. In a quite unique sense it is true to say that in Scotland today we have a National Church that is at once established and free, and of this we can be justly proud. It is not the purpose of this Section to trace the steps by which this has been achieved – some of the Answers on 'The Right to Differ' deal with this aspect of things – but merely to indicate some of the ways in which the relationship is manifested.

The answers on the Lord High Commissioner and on the Established Church seek to show, at the level of the Assembly on the one hand, and of the local congregation on the other, how the conflicting claims of Christ and Caesar have been resolved. It is all gathered together in a piece of legislation called the Declaratory Articles, at which we have already looked closely.

13

WHAT IS THE
LORD HIGH COMMISSIONER?

Seeing that we, by reason of our weighty affairs cannot in person be present in the said Assembly, and We having had full proof of the sufficiency and fidelity of Our Right Trusty and Right Well-Beloved Cousin A... B..., do by these presents

> *nominate, constitute and appoint A… B… to be our*
> *High Commissioner, Giving and Granting unto*
> *him full power, commission and warrant to represent*
> *our Sacred Person and Royal Authority in the said*
> *ensuing General Assembly.*

SO in its highly dignified, if both cumbersome, archaic, and fairly meaningless, language the Commission which the Purse-Bearer hands down from the Throne Gallery to be read by the Principal Clerk to a standing Assembly at the outset of that Court's first formal session. At the other end of the proceedings, once the final item of business has been concluded, the Moderator turns to face the Commissioner, extends thanks for his presence throughout the Assembly and his interest in its proceedings, ending with some such words as, 'and now, Your Grace, with affection and gratitude I bid you in the name of the General Assembly a respectful and dutiful farewell'. It used to be that the Commissioner at this point addressed the court, but that is no longer so.

Behind these simple ceremonial acts and these innocent-sounding phrases there lies a tale of years of antagonism and struggle.

Power to convene

The roots of the office of Lord High Commissioner lie very close to the heart of Presbyterianism itself. From the beginning of General Assemblies it was apparent that a vital question affecting the validity of any convention was whether it met with consent of the Crown. The Kirk had no objection to the Throne knowing what it was doing so long as no attempt was made to direct its business, interfere in its affairs, restrict its freedom. So the custom grew whereby the King sent a Commissioner to the Assembly with what amounted to a watching brief. Thus the astute Jamie the Saxt was able to interfere, if in a mild way. Only the King could convene the Assembly and it was he who determined when and where it was to meet. By an adroit management of these factors of time and place the wisest fool in Christendom was able to achieve many things detrimental to the absolute authority of the Kirk.

Power to dissolve

It was, of course, after Charles I succeeded to the throne that trouble really came to a head. At the famous Glasgow Assembly of 1638 the Marquis of Hamilton was King's Commissioner. No properly free Assembly had met for thirty years. There had been a preliminary skirmish on the question whether Elders were to attend. The much hated Bishops were to be facing some charges, and though these in some cases were trivial they were enough to sist the Bishops at the bar and so prevent them from speaking or voting. The scene was set for a stirring Assembly.

Having sat from 21st to 28th November dealing with preliminary business the Assembly reached, on the 29th, the trial of the Bishops. The Commissioner had done everything in his power to prevent things coming to this pass, and when it had become clear that he had failed he solemnly in name of the Sovereign dissolved the Assembly and himself withdrew, two Ministers and three Elders accompanying him. The other 235 members sat on – and on 20th December were still sitting on. If the Monarch had power to dissolve the Assembly whenever it proposed to do something that displeased him, the freedom of the Kirk didn't amount to much.

Power to intervene

Not only has the Sovereign from time to time claimed the right to call and dissolve Assemblies, he has also insisted he had the right to intervene in their affairs. This finally took the form of a struggle regarding what came to be known as 'the intrinsic power of the Church'. This issue was ultimately settled in favour of the Kirk when the Act ratifying the Treaty of Union of 1707 went on to secure the Protestant religion and the Presbyterian form of Church government 'to the people of the land in all succeeding generations', and also to require the Sovereign on his or her succession to swear to uphold that situation.

The Position Today

The present situation is that the Commissioner is still, as much as ever he was, appointed to supply the Sovereign's Royal Presence. He is housed in the royal palace of Holyroodhouse, his place of precedence puts him next to the Dukes of Edinburgh and Rothesay and before the other members of the Royal Family, the lion rampant standard is flown during his residence, he is known as 'Lord' and addressed as 'Your Grace', he is attended by the Solicitor General, and by the Dean of the Thistle and Chapel Royal. From the point of view of the Queen he quite definitely stands in her place.

But from the point of view of the Assembly he is very much an outsider. He sits in a gallery which is, strictly, outwith the Assembly and he addresses the court only when invited so to do. Instead of dissolving the one Assembly and appointing the next, he now undertakes to report to Her Majesty that the Assembly's business being over they have passed an Act fixing the date of their next meeting.

In 1969 the Queen attended the Assembly in person so no Commissioner was appointed. The following year she was pleased to appoint the Right Honourable Margaret Herbison PC as Commissioner, being the first woman to hold the office. Twenty-five years passed until in 1995

Marion Anne, Lady Fraser, wife of the Principal of Glasgow University, was appointed. The word 'Lord' has now been omitted from the title of the office, the holder being known simply as 'Her Majesty's Commissioner'.

14

WHAT IS AN ESTABLISHED CHURCH?

TO proclaim that the Church of Scotland is a Church by law established could at one time have been enough to stir up the proverbial hornet's nest. On the one side there are those who see in that phrase the mark of the Kirk's true greatness, the prize of years of struggle and suffering, a reference to the most perfect balance ever yet achieved between the conflicting claims upon man's allegiance of Church and State, the declaration that in our land we have discovered the formula by which it is possible to render unto Caesar the things that are Caesar's while reserving for God the things that are God's. On the other hand there are those who see in the idea of establishment the symbol of the Kirk's shame, servitude and apostasy, the chain that binds her in subservience, the evidence of her endeavour simultaneously to serve God and mammon.

Nor can there be any doubt that historically the issue of the relation between Church and State has been the question which, far beyond any other, has bitterly divided Presbyterians. Behind the problem of patronage that figures so large in the forefront of all the secessions lay the question as to what authority the courts of the land possessed entitling them to legislate in the Kirk's affairs, and that in turn was just another form of the question of whether man's first duty is to God or to the Crown.

Far removed as we are today from the passions

and prejudices of these old controversies, let us try to take a calm look at this question of what in Scotland we have come to mean when we speak of 'the established Church'.

Protected by the State

To say that the Church of Scotland is by law established might seem to mean that it is recognised and protected by the State. But it must mean more than that, for even the denomination that is most hostile to establishment can claim recognition and protection by the State. A Church is, at the lowest estimate, a voluntary association of citizens, and so long as its constitution is legal and it obeys its own rules and keeps the law, it will be protected by the State through the agency of the courts, civil and criminal.

What is special about the Church of Scotland that it alone has guaranteed to it, now and for all time, both its constitution and its right, within certain safeguards, itself to alter the constitution without reference to the State? Our Church, alone, of any institution in the land, religious or secular, has the right without the possibility of outside interference to manage its own affairs insofar as they are spiritual affairs.

When, back in the 1930s, certain members of a Church of Scotland congregation appealed to the Court of Session for permission to call a Minister, the case was dismissed not because that court was necessarily satisfied that the Presbytery had acted correctly in refusing permission but simply because they as a civil court had no power to review the actings of the Presbytery in such a matter – they had no jurisdiction.

There is, besides, the provision made in the Act of 1693 that 'magistrates, judges, and officers of justice must give all due assistance for making the sentences and censures of the Church and judicatories thereof to be obeyed'. In passing an order compelling a witness to attend a Church court, Lord President Inglis quoted the above and added, 'I want nothing stronger or more comprehensive than that. Whenever the Church courts are unable of themselves to carry out their own orders ... the civil courts are bound to step in and give all due assistance'.

That, of course, was away back in 1874. But it was fairly recently that a newspaper printed an account of a judicial proceeding which a Presbytery had taken in private. The editor, on legal advice, tendered a most abject apology, giving an undertaking that the offence would not be repeated.

These considerations, it must be noted, apply exclusively to the Church by law established.

Independent of the State

While there is this close link between the Church and State and the former enjoys the protection and active support of the latter, there is no subservience of Church to State. Completely foreign to our conception of establishment is the situation that obtains south of the border where the Church can change the text of the Prayer Book only through an Act of Parliament, and where appointments to high offices within the Church are made by the Queen on the personal advice of the Prime Minister.

Owing a Duty to the State

If the Church of Scotland enjoys special privileges, it carries also, as is most just, a special burden of responsibility. It is at once the privilege and the duty of the National Church to make the services of religion available for all, members and non-members, rich and poor, grateful and unappreciative alike. Ours is a parish Church not a group of congregational clubs. Our duty is that of providing a national spiritual health service.

A National Church such as ours has a duty too to act as the conscience of the nation. As the prophet of old had at times to take the king to task and remind him that he was the servant of a higher Lord, so it may well be the duty of the Kirk to take a stand for Christian principles against the leading of a government which is setting them at naught. It was in order that we might be free so to do that our fathers fought to establish the principle of the Headship of Christ.

In closing let it be said that by common consent it is agreed that in Scotland the problem of the relationship of Church and State has been as nearly perfectly solved as can ever be in this imperfect world and that in all Christendom there is no Church which can more truly claim to be established yet free.

15
WHAT IS A
PARISH QUOAD OMNIA?

THE term *quoad omnia* literally means 'in respect of everything', and it is to be distinguished from *quoad sacra* which means 'in respect of sacred things'. When the sacred things affecting a parish have been deducted from 'everything' you are left with civil matters, and if you want to refer to these in Latin you use the term *quoad civilia*. To be perfectly accurate the expression parish *quoad omnia,* when used in reference to a particular charge, is today properly an anachronism, for in our modern set-up no charge enjoys (or is burdened with according to how you see it) the extent and variety of responsibilities which the name implies. At the present time every charge of the Church of Scotland is a parish church, having under its spiritual oversight an area correctly described as its parish. Its full title, however, must be parish *quoad sacra*. This is true whatever may have been its pre-1929 affiliation, and indeed it is true of the Church Extension charge just granted full status – all of them alike are parishes in respect of sacred things.

Parish Administration

The situation derives from history, for in olden times the Church carried responsibility for many things which we should not now regard as ecclesiastical in any sense whatever and which we are happy to leave in care of the secular arm. The Church of Scotland after the Reformation – and indeed until less than a century ago – had through the machinery of its parish ministry to look after the poor, to provide facilities for education, to maintain a graveyard, to administer certain trust funds, and to be responsible for a variety of other things.

In due season these things passed out of the hands of the Kirk Session and Heritors as such, but the organisational unit represented by the parish was retained under the new system. Thus until the passing of local government legislation in the present century we continued to have things like the Parish Council, the Parish School Board, Parish Relief. That is to say, education and poor relief were still based upon the unit of the parish and constituted the civil aspect of parish administration.

At the same time that these matters of civil administration were growing in extent and importance, the Church was finding itself confronted with the necessity of creating new parishes to cope with the changed distribution of population consequent on the Industrial Revolution. At first this was met by the creation of what were little more than mission stations, though in the attempt to bestow upon them some little dignity they called them Chapels of Ease. They were not in any sense Parish Churches, their Ministers had no seats in Presbytery, they were without Kirk Sessions, their members' names appeared on the roll of the Parish Church, and in all matters of discipline their members were answerable to the Minister and Kirk Session of the Parish in which the Chapel was situated.

Parish Quoad Sacra

Clearly such a state of affairs could not continue. In many cases the new community had come to be larger and more important than the old – Wishaw in the Parish of Cambusnethan and Barrhead in that of Neilston spring readily to mind. It was clear that some way had to be found for creating new parishes. Such a way was in fact supplied by an Act of 1844, but its provisions were taken advantage of only to the extent of erecting ten new *quoad omnia* parishes, and none has been erected since. The Act, however, also provided for the erection of parishes *quoad sacra*. In these 'the Minister and Elders have the status and all the powers, rights and privileges of a Minister and Elders of the Church of Scotland'. From the purely ecclesiastical point of view there was no distinction between the two. But so far as the civil implications were concerned these were to remain unchanged, so that if a new parish of 'N' were to be created within the old parish of 'O' all the civil matters concerned with poor relief were to continue unchanged – that is to say squarely on the plate of congregation 'O'. It was not long ere 'O' was complaining that 'N' had taken away its income but left it with all the bills.

From a practical point of view today the only significant difference between a former *quoad omnia* parish and any other has to do with the mode of its internal government. Originally such a parish had heritors whose duty it was to build and maintain the church and manse and to provide the stipend. There was no need for local trustees for there was no property for them to hold, and no need for Managers for there were no funds for them to manage. Thus there was in the old *quoad omnia* congregation only a Kirk Session. As gradually the heritors dropped out of the picture the Kirk Session had to accept more and more of those responsibilities for temporal affairs that had been borne by the heritors so that today in most such cases the Kirk Session is wholly and solely responsible for all the material affairs of the congregation – as well as for the spiritual oversight of the parish.

Historical Significance

Even though it be agreed that the name parish *quoad omnia* has lost all legal point and significance, it is still meaningful in an historical context. For it reminds us of a time – which is all too easy to forget – when the Kirk in Scotland was the one and only body which concerned itself either with the provision of education or with the relief of poverty. And in this connection it is well to remember that the 'poor relief' had a wider connotation than either 'benevolent fund' or 'parish assistance'. Poverty may result from a variety of causes (unemployment, illness, accident, congenital infirmity, widowhood, old age), all the things in fact for which today the Welfare State makes provision in one or another branch of what we have come to call 'social security'.

In the early nineteenth century there was no acceptance by the State of any obligation (beyond the provision of a poors' house) to relieve the poor, the needy, and the fatherless. But there was a Church that accepted a duty in this connection. Its resources were sadly limited, its machinery utterly inadequate, its provision pitifully small. But it did accept a burden which no other would bear, and in due course brought the State to an awareness of its obligation in this field.

16
WHO WERE
THE HERITORS?

YOU cannot say anything about the Kirk in Scotland in the eighteenth/nineteenth centuries without constant reference to 'the heritors'. Who were they? The short answer is that they were the owners of heritable property within the bounds. In virtue of such land-ownership they owed certain obligations towards the Kirk, as well as enjoying certain privileges in relation to it.

Obviously between one parish and another the number of heritors could vary enormously. In a country parish all of the land could be in possession of one, perhaps two, maybe three, large landowners, every house and farm in the parish being the property of one of them. In a residential community, on the other hand, there could be within a single parish hundreds, even thousands, of heritors, each the feuar of a plot of ground on which stood his own house, business or factory.

The reason for the connection between these people and the Kirk was that at the Reformation, and the years after, the vast resources of the then Church had been appropriated by the Crown, nobles and certain local authorities. Out of the wealth that had thus passed from the ownership of the Kirk, certain provisions had been made for the maintenance of religion. These were a burden on the fruits of the land and went with the land. So when someone took a feu, he accepted not only an obligation towards his feudal superior in the form of a feu-duty, but also a share of the latter's responsibility for the provision of the ordinances of religion within the parish.

Duties of the Heritors

One of the principal duties of the heritors was to pay the stipend, which was assessed in terms of grain, as explained more fully in later answers. A manse with suitable offices and garden had to be provided, as well as either a glebe which varied in extent but was of not less than four acres Scots (five imperial acres), or 'minister's grass', which might vary in location from one year to the next but must be enough to graze one horse and two cows. It was also laid upon the heritors to set aside ground for a burial place for the parish, though in this case the land involved continued to be held by them, but in trust.

The burden which probably caused most trouble was that of providing and maintaining a church capable of seating two-thirds of the 'examinable persons' in the parish – that is, those of 18 years and upwards. Not only had the building to conform thus in size, it had to be made safe and healthy and such that the congregation might worship in it in reasonable comfort. Over the years, needless to say, decisions were often sought in the courts as to what precisely was meant by terms such as the above. Often too there were disputes on matters such as the following: a vestry is an indispensable part of a church; heating provided by a modern system is necessary for the reasonable comfort of the worshippers; furniture for the Sacraments, bowls and lavers for Baptism, 'cups, tables and table-clothes' for the Lord's Supper are essential; bell and a belfry must be provided; steeple is not essential, but if one is there it must be cared for.

New Church at Shettleston

As will be deduced from the above, the heritors did not always take either kindly or very seriously their duty of maintaining a church, and they often sought to fulfil it in the least expensive manner possible, though it should be emphasised that this was not by any means the universal rule and that we owe many very fine pieces of architecture to the conscientious care of heritors. So long as a parish had a principal heritor, 'the laird', with a sense of responsibility for the overall well-being of the community all was likely to be well. When, however, the heritors were a hetergeneous collection of small feuars, many of them not connected in any way with the church (some even hostile to it) and who in most cases when they bought or sold their houses had imagined the full extent of their obligation lay in the payment of a few shillings annually for stipend – in such a case the requirement to build a new church, or very substantially to repair and enlarge an old one, could raise a storm.

An example of this which became a *cause célèbre* was Shettleston, which had been created a parish *quoad omnia* in 1847. This district at that time was growing impressively even as the fabric of the old Kirk deteriorated relentlessly. Mr John White (later of much fame) went there as a young man in 1893 to find a building which nearly ten years earlier had been declared by the Presbytery to be in a serious state of disrepair. He set himself the task of having a new church built – a task to which he held steadfastly in face of many difficulties and discouragements.

For years the battle raged between congregation and heritors. In the end, John White won the day and a new church was built for Shettleston.

It was as late as 1929 that the last case of the kind arose when a new church had to be built – in Cathcart this time to the no small chagrin of the many owners of small houses in that parish. This particular chapter has now been closed by the Church of Scotland (Property and Endowments) Act.

In acknowledgment of their responsibilities in maintaining the church, the heritors enjoyed certain privileges. They were entitled to sittings in the church, and in the case of the large land-owners it was not unusual for a whole gallery (or 'laft') to be set aside for their use, the front pew, suitably furnished with easy chairs, being reserved for the laird and his family and guests, those immediately behind for servants, and others for tenants.

The principal privilege, of course, was the right of patronage, the power to present 'the living' to the person of his choice. This right, generally, was enjoyed by the principal heritor, latterly a privilege of doubtful worth to the owner and a cause of great unhappiness to the Church.

In the Scotland of the eighteenth century there was a real place for the heritor; by the nineteenth that place was highly insecure; by the twentieth it was untenable. The Act of 1874 abolishing patron-age came far too late; the Act of 1925 affecting property came not a day too soon. We have had a lot for which to thank the heritors; we should be glad we don't have to thank them any more.

17
WHAT WAS PATRONAGE?

PATRONAGE must have been the most vexa-tious thing ever to afflict the Kirk in Scotland.

The idea was of very ancient origin. It was quite usual for a cause to be established by some wealthy landowner to serve his staff and retainers, and reasonably enough since he was footing all the bills he reserved to himself the right of choosing the incumbent. So there came to be established the idea that the chief landowner of a parish, being responsible for a large share of the expense of maintaining the charge, should have the right of presenting to it. When burghs began to grow in size and statute laid it upon them to erect and endow charges, they too were given the right to present. The system seemed eminently fair, and it is probably true that it resulted in no more and no worse misfits than any subsequent system of popular election! But principles are principles.

In any case it was protected by two provisions – first of all that the congregation had the opportunity of backing up the appointment with a 'Call', and second that the Presbytery had to take the presentee on trials to satisfy itself that he was qualified for the appointment.

Patronage had in fact been abolished in the time of Presbytery's temporary triumph in 1649, but immediately Episcopacy returned to power in 1660 it was restored. Then (see Answer on the Revolution Settlement, page 42) occasion was taken in 1690 to have patronage finally abolished. King William was none too keen, but gave way on the point so that an Act was passed whereby in all vacancies Heritors and Elders were to nominate a person for the approval of the congregation. Should that body have any fault to find, they were to state this to the Presbytery by whom the matter would finally be settled. In consideration of being deprived of a valuable right, the patron was to receive a sum of 600 merks. This new system did not commend itself and compensation was paid in only two cases.

Restoration of Patronage

The two Parliaments were united in 1707 and it was at Westminster that new parliamentary legislation affecting the Kirk was to originate. In 1712 the Toleration Act allowed Episcopacy to celebrate its rites – as was no more than bare justice, long delayed at that. But the Tory government which pushed the Act through was known to be set upon the restoration of the Stuart dynasty and the Act was generally seen as part of a deep-dyed plot and looked upon with grave suspicion in consequence. In particular Scottish Presbyterians saw it as a foretaste of the treatment they might expect from Westminster.

They had not long to wait to have their fears ratified, for in that same year (1712) an Act was passed restoring patronage. Nor can there be any doubt but that it was instigated by the Jacobite party with a view to the return of Episcopacy. Of this Act, Lord Macaulay, in a speech in the House of Commons in 1845, had this to say:

> In 1712 Tory statesmen were in power: Tory squires formed more than 5/6 th of this House. The guarantee so solemnly given to the Church of Scotland [in 1707] was a subject of loud and bitter complaint. The Ministers hated that Church, and their chief supporters, the country gentlemen of England hated it still more. It was determined to go further and to restore to the old patrons those rights which had been taken away in 1690. A Bill passed through this House before the people of Scotland knew that it had been brought in. For there were then neither reporters nor railroads, and intelligence from West-minster was longer in travelling to Cambridge than it now is travelling to Aberdeen. The Bill was in the House of Lords before the Church of Scotland could make her voice heard. Carstares and his colleagues appealed to the Act of Union and implored the peers not to violate that Act. But party spirit ran high: patronage was restored. To that breach of the Treaty of Union are to be ascribed all the schisms that have since rent the Church of Scotland.

Cause of Secession

Later Answers trace in detail the steps leading to

the Secessions of 1733 and 1761 and to the Disruption of 1843. Suffice it to say here that all of them were triggered off by the operation of Patronage. In fact the hostility to patronage when restored in 1712 was not so violent as it was later to become. Many patrons, conscious of the ill-will likely to be generated were they to exercise their right, no matter how fairly, were allowing the appointment to fall to the Presbytery. And strictly it was over a question of just how Presbytery were to exercise their power in such cases that there began the series of events destined to culminate at Gairney Bridge in 1733 with the creation of the Associate Synod.

The connection between Patronage and the Second Secession was more direct. The Assembly had ordained that the Presbytery of Dunfermline was to attend at Inverkeithing on a certain day to induct a presentee much resisted by the congregation. Fewer than a quorum appeared. It was as leader of the rebel group of absentees that Thomas Gillespie was deposed and the course set for the meeting at Colinsburgh in 1761 that formed the Relief Church.

The Disruption was closely enough linked with patronage. The Church had tried to find ways around the hated system but had invariably been thwarted by the judgement of some civil court, so that much of the hatred had been diverted from patronage to what was seen as the improper intervention of the civil courts in the Kirk's domestic affairs.

It was not until 1874 that patronage was finally abolished and disappeared for ever – though it certainly could not be said to have disappeared without trace, for it left this pathetic heritage of schism and bitterness.

Two questions linger in the mind. First, did the system work really badly, or was it just hated for its own sake? And second had there been no such thing as the Law of Patronage would not divisions still have occurred within the Scottish Kirk of that period?

18

WHAT IS A POOR'S FUND?

THERE must be few congregations in Scotland which do not have a Session Benevolent Fund or similar provision (by whatever name) from which – usually around Christmas – small sums of money, or hampers of groceries are distributed among pensioners and needy invalids within the congregation. This modest fund, which today probably gives more embarrassment in its administration than help in its application, is the survival of the old Poor's Fund which, surprisingly enough, was the most important item in all the congregations accounts, and upon whose benefactions many depended for their very survival.

To the Scottish Reformers the duty of caring for the poor lay at the very heart of the Christian Gospel. The First Book of Discipline (1560) enjoined that 'every several Kirk Session must provide for the poor within itself'. Apart from the exercise of discipline there was no more urgent or important duty laid upon a Session than that of sustentation of the poor, and to the latter no less than to the former the average Kirk Session devoted itself with zeal and earnestness. It is a pity indeed that their efforts in the one direction have not attracted a measure of appreciation comparable to the notoriety which their labours in the other have achieved.

The Beneficiaries

It has to be appreciated that the Poor's Fund operated by the Kirk Session of an earlier day was something vastly different from either the

Benevolent Fund or Public Assistance today. The former exists to give a little extra to deserving cases where there is stringency, the latter to ensure that relief will be available where there is utter need, no matter whether the result of misfortune or of improvidence. The contingencies of life which normally result in poverty are today taken care of by a series of State Insurance Schemes – unemployment, sickness, disablement, industrial injury, widowhood are provided for in this way. So accustomed have we become to this state of affairs that we find it hard to believe that the oldest of these ameliorative measures was National Health Insurance introduced as comparatively recently as 1912. Prior to that a person might be poor because of these or similar chances and it was the Kirk and the Kirk alone that was in the business of caring for him or her.

Sources of Income

To meet these many needs the Scottish Kirk had a variety of sources from which it drew an income. First, was the collection taken at the Church door or kirkyard gate at every regular service. About this subject generally more will be found in the Answer on The Collection (see page 90). By modern standards these offerings were trifling amounts, but one has to remember that by any standard the people who were contributing to the support of the poor were themselves living precariously near the bread-line. An interesting feature, though, is the amount of doubtful coinage that found its way into the Church plate. Any set of accounts of the eighteenth century has an entry regarding 'sale of bad copper' – in one case in 1748 for example, a sum of £43.19.7 of bad copper fetched £7.17.6. It is true to say that in those days a lot of doubtful currency was in circulation, but one feels the Kirk must have got more than its fair share.

The second main source of income was the assessment or 'stent' – being the Scots word for stretch. As early as 1579 an Act of Parliament ordained magistrates 'to tax or stent the whole inhabitants according to the estimate of their substance, in such weekly charges as shall be thought expedient for the sustentation of the poor of the parish'. Unfortunately those in authority were unwilling to exercise this power to any meaningful extent, and in consequence the freewill offerings of the people had to be correspondingly greater. After the Industrial Revolution a realistic enforcement of the stent upon larger employers (as was urged in vain by many a parish minister) could have provided the basis for a system of insurance against the unemployment so likely to overtake the workers.

Imposition of Fines

A third source of revenue lay in fines – those exacted by the Kirk Session for some forms of delinquency as well as certain penalties imposed by the civil courts. Of these the latter are still exigible today – but in practice actions would not be raised in respect of them. They include, for example, the Act for the Due Observance of the Sabbath Day, which prohibits 'all Salmond-fishing, going of Salt pans, Mills or Kilnes, all Hyring of Shearers, carrying of Loads, keeping of Mercats, or using any sort of Merchandisse on the said day, and all other prophanation thereof whatsoever'. If the poor of today had to await relief till a conviction was secured under this Act his poverty would be of long duration.

More interesting perhaps were the ecclesiastical fines. There were fines for clandestine marriage, for absolution from fornication, for irregularities of one sort and another, such as being proclaimed on one Sunday instead of three, and for private (or chamber) baptism. In 1763 a woman appeared before the Kirk Session at Kilmarnock and confessed that in wrath and haste she had said, 'The devill ryd to hell on James Thomson and leave the horse behind him'. For this gracious sentiment she had, among other things, to subscribe thirty shillings to the Poor's Fund.

There were some other sources of income, such as the bell-penny, a charge for the ringing or tolling of the bell at funerals; the hire of the mort-cloth – also at funerals; and the surrender of the consigation money for marriages. (See next Answer on Proclamation, page 72).

From the outset, as has been indicated, it was envisaged that each parish would be responsible for its own poor. This, which on the face of it seemed fair enough, led in practice to considerable hardship, for it put a premium on being able to prove the pauper was not your responsibility. One record refers to a sum paid to two strong men for 'removing' a pauper to his proper parish. By mid eighteenth century there was considerable vagrancy encouraged by this insistence that each parish should be responsible for its own poor.

A further difficulty resulting from the practice of administering poor relief on a strictly parish basis was that where vast numbers of people had been lured into a district because work was plentiful in the new mills these people might attach themselves to the Secession Churches or to the parish *quoad sacra*, but it was the parish *quoad omnia* which had to support them when, as so often happened, unemployment struck. This manifest injustice was never fairly tackled.

It is good that today the Parish Church should not have to carry the responsibility for the relief of poverty within its bounds. But it is well to remember that for so long the Kirk did manfully bear this burden, and to realise that if the Session Benevolent Fund has no great future it has at least an honourable past.

19
WHAT WAS THE
PROCLAMATION OF BANNS?

There is a purpose of marriage between A... A...
Bachelor, and B... B... Spinster, of which procla-
mation is hereby fully and finally made.

HOW accustomed we once were to hearing these
words read at the beginning of the 'intimations' at
Morning Service. Since 1978 it is most unlikely
that they have been so heard. What was this business of proclamation? Why should it have
occurred in Church, and that only in the Church
of Scotland? And why should it have ceased?

Until 1977 the formalities connected with
getting married were regulated by the terms of
the Marriage (Scotland) Act of 1939, which had
continued religious marriage, created civil
marriage (marriage by an Authorised Registrar)
and had done away with irregular marriage
except the case of 'habit and repute'. It required
that all marriages, whether religious or civil,
should be preceded by some form of publicity –
either Proclamation of Banns in a Parish Church
or Publication of Notice on a Registrar's notice-
board – but allowed that in circumstances of
emergency a licence might be obtained from the
Sheriff. This last was a novelty of the 1939 Act;
Publication had been authorised by an Act of
1878; Proclamation was of very ancient origin.

Meaning of Banns

Since long before the Reformation, regular
marriages in Scotland had always been preceded
by an intimation publicly read in church and
known as 'banns'. The word itself is derived from
Ecclesiastical Latin and means simply 'proclamation', so the phrase proclamation of banns is

strictly autonomous but is now fortified by long usage so that it has become part of the language. Contrary to common belief it has nothing to do with banning the wedding by alleging some impediment. To provide an opportunity for such an objection to be stated is the purpose of the exercise, but is not the meaning of the word.

The term too has to be distinguished from one of similar sound – bands of marriage. The word 'band' was in common use in Scotland to denote a covenant or contract – people banded themselves together for all kinds of objects, so that the term bands of marriage was to be equated with the more usual 'marriage bond'.

Putting in the Banns

In earliest usage the putting in of the banns was regarded as a kind of espousal and became in consequence an occasion of no small importance. Life in seventeenth/eighteenth century Scotland must have been a drab affair of unremitting toil, so that people would make the most of what few opportunities for relaxation came their way.

At one time it was required that the banns be put in at a regular Session meeting so that if an Elder knew of any impediment the banns need never be read at all. Later the plan was that the Minister was available at definite times to receive banns and it was enough if the couple brought with them 'the elder of their quarter'. Later still the duty of receiving the bann fell to the Session Clerk, the fee for proclamation being his perquisite. It was then that the occasion came to be thought of not so much as a time for solemn examination as rather opportunity for jollification, so that often the night when the young man and his friends went 'to see the schule-maister aboot pittin in the cries' would indeed be one to be long remembered, the contemporary equivalent of a stag party!

Consignation Money

At the same time the banns were put in, there had also to be lodged a sum of 'consignation money' – usually around £5, a lot of money in those days. Either this had to be laid on the table or a bond of caution had to be produced in respect of it. There would seem to have been a two-fold reason for this. For one thing it was to ensure that the couple would in fact marry within the three months of the validity of the Proclamation Certificate. Why the Kirk should have concerned itself with this is hard to understand, but then banns were a kind of betrothal so that forfeiture of the sum became a kind of fine for breach of promise.

The other purpose was to ensure that the couple would be wed 'without scandal'. What constituted 'scandal' may be apparent from the following – in 1658 Renfrew Kirk Session ordained that whoever had a piper playing at his wedding would forfeit his consignation; the Fenwick Kirk Session in 1647 restricted the number of persons who might attend to forty on each side, the penalty for breach being half the consignation; at Dumbarton in 1620 it was resolved that the most to be spent at a wedding was 'fyve schilling', with the penalty as before. Not many bridegrooms of today could hope to recover much of their consignation money.

Fully and Finally

Latterly in most congregations banns were proclaimed only once, the statement being added that proclamation was being fully and finally made, or occasionally that proclamation was being made 'for the first, second and third time'. This was harking back to a day when banns had to be called on three separate occasions. At least that was the rule. But exceptions were allowed.

There were those who didn't want to wait so long, or who disliked the large measure of extended publicity, or who for some reason wanted to get it all over in one or at worst two Sundays. This was seen as an irregularity involving the payment of a fine. The Session Clerk continued to collect the modest normal fee (usually half-a-crown) as his personal perquisite, while the fine proper (a much larger sum) was devoted to pious purposes – that is, it went to augment the Poor's Fund. So the odd situation obtained that to be 'cried' on one Sunday could cost you £1, but you could have it done three times over for 2/6d inclusive!

It is doubtful whether, outside rural parishes, proclamation ever served any very useful purpose from the point of view of publicity. The day may not be far away when we shall all at birth be registered on some glorified computer memory system that will keep track of all our movements, including our incursions into the field of matrimony. When marriage is in our mind we shall apply to the Registrar who will press the appropriate key and get for us a clear title in the form of an Eligibility Certificate.

It was with such a general idea in mind regarding the future that the General Assembly in 1978 agreed that proclamation had served its day and generation and should be discontinued – and passed legislation accordingly. It has to be said that there is no evidence that the incidence of bigamy has increased in consequence.

MANAGING THE
TEMPORAL AFFAIRS

THE ways in which the temporal affairs of congregations of the Church of Scotland are administered are many and varied, depending as they do upon the historical tradition from which the congregation springs.

The mention of Deacons points instantly to roots in the Free Church of 1843; talk of Managers and of a Preses takes us back to one of those Secession groups which in 1847 made common cause as the United Presbyterian Church; the possession of a Congregational Board opens up a number of possibilities – this congregation may have been erected as a parish *quoad sacra*, having perhaps begun life as a Church Extension charge, or it may be the product of a union of congregations which had been operating under different constitutions, or it may be a congregation that freely elected to adopt this method of doing things. There is a further possibility, the charge may be a former *quoad omnia* where the Kirk Session is responsible for the oversight of all the congregation's affairs, material as well as spiritual.

Under this general heading too there might be included something on the subjects of the Collection and of Seat Rents, the twin sources of revenue upon which the 'temporal affairs' depended.

20
WHAT IS A QUOAD OMNIA CONSTITUTION?

IN a steady, decreasing number of cases, congregations are still operating under the system which emerged, for want of any better, when the heritors disappeared from the scene in the old parishes *quoad omnia*. In these cases the Kirk Session has overall responsibility. Frequently you will hear this referred to (usually by Ministers) as 'the old', or maybe 'the good old', or perchance 'the traditional' method in the Kirk. This suggestion of hoary antiquity is a myth that should be exploded. It is true that in the early days there was one and one only ruling body in each congregation, and that, of course, was the Kirk Session. But these were days when the question of paying the Minister and of maintaining the property did not arise locally since they were being taken care of by the heritors; nor had the Elders to be worried about meeting bills for heating, lighting and insurance since they depended upon nature for light and heat and on the Almighty for insurance-cover. Nor did they have to find money to send to '121' since there was no '121' and there were no 'Schemes'. A day of bliss, you might think!

The Kirk Session of the last century Scottish parish – as the most cursory inspection of their minutes will reveal – devoted their whole attention to matters spiritual, especially to matters of discipline, and were not concerned with questions of ways and means. They were, certainly, responsible for the weekly collections and for the employment of these in support of the poor (see Answer on Poor's Fund on page 68) – and, no matter how the finances are administered the Kirk Session is still to this day in charge of the Benevolent Fund behind whatever name it hides.

It was only as the heritors faded from the scene and the amount of purely domestic expenditure increased that the need emerged for a body that would deal with these essentially temporal matters. By this time the business of discipline was diminishing in its demands, not because morals were markedly improving but because the Sessions were losing the sanctions they used to have to their hand, and so the Kirk Session of the old parish took on these, for them completely new, duties. But that didn't make the system either old or traditional.

Kirk Session Autonomy

The assumption of these new duties raises a quite serious constitutional problem that has yet to be seriously faced. For a Kirk Session is not, cannot be made, and should not be allowed to appear, answerable to the congregation – things are the other way round. It is of the essence of the Presbyterian system that answerability is always upward to the next superior court. The Kirk Session is answerable to the Presbytery and if, as a member of a congregation, you have some complaint against the Session, it is to the Presbytery you must go.

When a Kirk Session administers the finances, issues a balance sheet, calls a meeting of the congregation to receive reports, it puts itself in an awkward, not to say anomalous, position. One possibility is that it will invite questions, encourage discussion, and open up criticisms of its activities and intromissions – and thus seem to be making itself answerable to the congregation. The next step in this progression is for someone in course of the Annual Meeting to move that the Kirk Session be instructed to do something or other.

The other possibility is that the Moderator of Session will discourage any serious discussion of the balance-sheet, will evade answering questions, will refuse to accept instructions about future spending. In the one case the meeting becomes unconstitutional; in the other it becomes farcical – and in either case the Kirk Session can find itself in a most awkward and invidious position.

There is, of course, the other possibility of not holding a congregational meeting at all. A better way of creating unconcern it would be hard to find. The funds have been contributed by the congregation and the congregation is entitled to an accounting.

It is neither accident nor coincidence that as a general rule (and with some notable exceptions) congregations operating under the old *quoad omnia* constitution are at the bottom of the league so far as liberality is concerned, while those whose constitution puts responsibility for financial matters squarely on the shoulders of the people, encouraging them to take an interest in and reach decisions on these matters, are characterised by a higher level of generosity.

21
WHAT IS A
'UP' CONSTITUTION?

A UP constitution consists of the regulations for managing the temporal affairs of some particular congregation of the former United Presbyterian Church. Essentially it is a system wherein the management of all financial matters is undertaken by a body of Managers elected from the congregation by the congregation and answerable to the congregation. This Committee of Management operates under the chairmanship of a Preses, chosen in some cases by the congregation, in others by the Managers themselves. There is no provision for inclusion in its number of either Minister or Elders and though these may strictly by law be eligible for election the tradition must be almost universal that they have as a matter of principle to be excluded.

The Annual Meeting of the congregation at which the Managers give an account of their stewardship is opened with prayer by the Minister who is then expected to take his departure. In the event of a Manager being ordained to the Eldership, he is expected to resign from the Managers. They are under no obligation to confer with the Minister or Session on any matters falling within their remit. All of which has led to a tendency on the part of the Managers to be most jealous of their preserves.

Properly to understand this constitution and to appreciate its character we have to acquaint ourselves with something of the history of the UP Church, a body which came into being in 1847 with the union of United Secession and Relief denominations. Within these bodies constitutions of this kind had for long been in operation. What happened at the union was that a Model was prepared and recommended for general adoption. Each congregation, though, has still its own – there is a Model Deed but no Standard Deed.

The First Secession

As related in the Answers on Calls and on Anti-burghers (see pages 106, 151) the passing by the Assembly of 1832 of an Act anent Calls, and more particularly the reaction to this on the part of Ebenezer Erskine, led to a heated controversy in the Kirk. For eight years the battle raged, during which time four recalcitrant Ministers, though suspended, continued in their parishes and their pulpits while at the same time constituting themselves an 'Associate Synod'. Ultimately, in 1740, the Assembly felt compelled to take action against Ministers who while continuing to work in their parishes, live in their manses, draw their stipends, were carrying on a battle with authority, openly defying the judgments and censures of courts to which they had solemnly sworn allegiance. And so sentence of deposition was passed. Thus the Associate Synod was regularised as the Church of the First Secession.

The Second Secession

Twelve years later, on 22nd October 1761, under not dissimilar circumstances, Thomas Gillespie, Minister at Carnock, who had defied the specific orders of the Assembly to attend an Induction, was deposed.

Gillespie met at Colinsburgh in Fife with two others of like mind, Collier and Boston, and together the three of them constituted themselves the Presbytery of Relief, a denomination that grew considerably in importance so that by 1847 it numbered 118 charges. This breach is generally referred to as the Second Secession.

In regard to both of these movements it must be recognised that the Ministers concerned were not lone voices but rather were the mouthpieces of popular movements of considerable force and significance. Thus when a new meeting place was established it provided a focal-point for many who for one reason or another were uneasy and discontented in the Establishment.

Devising a Constitution

Two massive problems immediately confronted a body of people determined to form themselves into such a congregation. These were the provision of heritable properties (Church, Halls and Manse) and the finding of stipend. In these matters they had no precedents to guide them – the heritors had taken care of these mundane affairs. It does not seem to have occurred to these groups of Seceders to entrust such matters to the

Kirk Session, they being busy enough with spiritual concerns.

In their perplexity they conceived a new body to take care of these material things – a body not unlike the heritors whose duties they were in effect taking over. They were to be 'Managers'. In the first instance, no doubt, they would be, by and large, men of some substance – for without a few such it must have been near impossible to meet the heavy financial demands involved. It was their duty to act both as trustees for the property and as administrators of temporal affairs. To ensure, however, that they would do so within clearly-defined limits a constitution was prepared setting very strict limits to their powers. This was the UP Constitution and in its detail differed from one congregation to the next.

In modern days it is true to say there are many cases where this constitution works extraordinarily well – some of the best giving and most efficiently organised congregations operate it – but in fairness it has also to be said it has been responsible for some of the most unhappy situations in the relation of Minister and Officebearers. Its essential weakness lies in the too clear-cut, too sharp, distinction it wants to draw between temporal and spiritual, and in its failure adequately to bring these together. Every spiritual experience in life has its material expression; even the most material objects have their spiritual undertones. This is a fact which we ignore at our peril.

The number of congregations operating under one of these constitutions is steadily shrinking, but those that remain are very jealous of their position and generally very proud too that 'we hold our own titles'. They cling tenaciously to the spirit of independence out of which their denominations sprang.

An interesting feature of every UP Constitution is that it closes with a clause saying that nothing in the foregoing is to interfere with what it describes as 'the constitutional right of the Kirk Session to call a congregational meeting'. It has always seemed to the writer that this confrontation of two 'constitutions' represents a strange phenomenon. Should not the so-called UP Constitution be seen simply as a set of rules for managing the temporal affairs of former UP congregations?

22
WHAT IS
A DEACONS' COURT?

THE office of Deacon has its origin in Scripture. In classical Greek the word *diakonos* meant a servant, but not a bond servant. The term, however, acquired a new significance in virtue of the events recorded in Acts 6. From its very earliest days the Christian Church was what we now call a caring Church, making provision for the material no less than for the spiritual needs of its people. As can so easily happen in such a case, problems arose in Jerusalem, the Greeks complaining that the Jewish widows were enjoying preferential treatment. The Apostles, confronted with the question of what should be done, took the view that their calling was to preach the Gospel – they had no time to be 'serving tables'.

They accordingly ordained that seven men should be chosen, 'of good repute, full of the spirit and of wisdom' to take charge of this whole sphere of activity. The seven were chosen and the Apostles laid their hands on them in prayer. These were the Deacons. It is worth noting that their being seconded to this task did not, apparently, debar their preaching, for Stephen and Philip both distinguished themselves in this direction, but they did so as individuals and not as part of their diaconal duty.

In 1843 occurred that great secession from the Established Church known as the Disruption, when some 450 Ministers left Manse and livelihood behind them in the cause of freedom from State control. Literally they went out not knowing – financially at least – whither they went. In this respect the Disruption differed from the earlier secessions. In these cases groups of likeminded people had formed themselves into praying societies which gradually grew to become congregations able to call and to support a Minister. It was a process of natural development. The Disruption, on the other hand, was a catastrophic event whereby some hundreds of Ministers and congregations at a stroke found themselves to be jobless and homeless.

It was largely due to the genius – and faith – of one man, Thomas Chalmers, that this massive transition took place without tragedy resulting. When it had become apparent that a parting of the ways was inevitable Chalmers convened in November 1842 a meeting of Ministers and Elders likely to be interested in cutting themselves off from the Establishment and put it to them that it would be morally wrong as well as financially unrealistic to expect that Ministers who came out would be supported by their people who came out with them. Even if the whole congregation adhered to its Minister the experience of having to support him financially would be a complete novelty. Chalmers proposed, therefore, that an annual fund be set up to take the place of the endowments of the *quoad sacra* parishes. The stipend of these charges stood at that time at £120 and it was his idea that an annual income of about £54,000 would be needed if this level of stipend was to be available. Set against the prevailing standard of congregational liberality the figure was nothing short of astronomical and there were not wanting those who dubbed Chalmers' vision an idle dream.

No one had anything better to suggest, and before the Disruption had taken place 'associations' were being set up in many parts of the country to whip up enthusiasm and to set up machinery. In the event, in the first year of its existence this new Sustentation Fund, as it was called, brought in £68,704 instead of the £54,000 that had been laughed out of court, and within ten years it had reached the £100,000 mark – all of it new money. An incredible achievement.

The Deacons' Court

It was primarily to advance the cause of the Sustentation Fund that the Free Church adopted the office of Deacon. Each family within the new denomination received a monthly visit from their Deacon in the interests of the Fund. Apart from its financial implications, there can be no doubt that this system of faithful visitation by the Deacons strengthened the hand of both Minister and Elders in the pastoral care of the people and may go farther than is generally recognised to explain the success that attended the new denomination in those early formative years.

Each congregation of the Free Church had a Deacons' Court in charge of its temporal affairs, and this continued into the UF Church and still obtains today in most congregations of this tradition. The Court is made up of the Minister, the Elders, and the Deacons, the last-named being persons elected by the congregation for this duty. The Session decides when an election of Deacons is called for, and how many there should be, the original principle being that there should be a Deacon to offset every Elder. The Minister is Chairman of the Court, though in his absence any member may be chosen to preside. It is not uncommon for there to be a number of

Treasurers each in charge of some specific fund. Generally the Court meets monthly, and while for some special reason it may resolve to hold an open meeting it normally meets in private.

The original pattern followed the Scripture warrant in that Deacons were ordained and accordingly held office for life or until leaving the congregation. Ordination is not so common today. They were, of course, subject to the discipline of the Kirk Session.

Changing Pattern

A number of factors are today conspiring to change the character of the Deacons' Court so that it corresponds more and more closely with the Congregational Board of the Model Deed.

For some time the office has been open to women. Provision has also existed whereby the congregation may decide that instead of the Deacons being ordained they should be elected for a three year stint. In recent years this alternative method has gained in popularity so today fewer and fewer Deacons are being ordained. As a result the distinctive status of the office is in peril.

Other factors have had their effects, for one thing the introduction of the Weekly Freewill Offering system of giving (WFO); and for another the new arrangements governing payment of stipend and giving to Schemes have so revolutionised congregational finance that there is no longer any place for the Deacon as a monthly visitor and collector. So his distinctive function has gone as well.

Whatever the future may hold in store for the Deacons' Court the Free Kirk over the years has been enormously indebted to its Deacons for the part they have played in carrying it successfully through the most critical years of its history.

23
WHAT IS
THE MODEL CONSTITUTION?

DURING the early days of Church Extension, when the Kirk was frantically trying to cope with the problems created by the Industrial Revolution, Chapels of Ease were springing up with remarkable speed in many parts of the country. Before such a cause could achieve the status of a Parish *quoad sacra* certain conditions had to be fulfilled. There had to be a building; there had to be (in feu duties and ground annuals) enough capital to endow a stipend of £120; and there had to be a constitution for the conduct of affairs acceptable to the Presbytery. At first, as was to be expected, though the constitutions covered the same ground there was plenty of variety in the detail of the patterns produced and no standard form was compulsory.

These deeds of constitution made provision for the heritable property to be held by trustees (usually local), for the appointment of managers (who might be or might include, the trustees), and for their giving account to the congregation. An interesting feature of most was that any balance at credit of the ordinary account at the end of the year went to the Minister as supplement to stipend, though in some cases a certain limited percentage was creamed off towards a sinking fund for fabric.

Like so many other things in the management of the Kirk the position of the *quoad sacra* parish was reviewed following on the Union of 1929, so that in 1931 an Act was passed setting forth a Model Deed of Constitution for Parishes *quoad sacra* – a model which was to govern the matter for the next 34 years. It was to apply to all existing *quoad sacra* charges; it was to be issued to all new charges created within the united Church; it could be issued on application to any congregation which wished to adopt it on condition that its heritable property was conveyed into the name of the General Trustees; and in cases of readjustment, where uniting congregations had operated under different deeds, it was usually written into the Basis of Union that they would adopt the Model Deed. In one way and another before long the Model Deed was in fairly general use.

It required that there be a Stated Meeting of the congregation held not later than 31st March after two Sundays notice from the pulpit. At this meeting there should be elected certain members to act along with the Kirk Session as the Congregational Board. The total was not to exceed the number of Elders at the date of election, and they were to be appointed for a period of three years, being eligible for re-election immediately thereafter. The Minister was Chairman *ex officio* though he was free to decline office, and in that case the Board itself elected one of its number to act for the year. The Board also appointed a Clerk one of whose duties was to keep a minute of the Stated Meeting. And of course it appointed a Treasurer to take charge of its funds.

The Board was responsible for all financial affairs with the exception of the Poor's Fund which remained with the Session, and any trust fund where other conditions were specified. It was responsible for: (a) payment of stipend (declared to be a 'first charge on ordinary revenue'); (b) all expenses necessarily incurred in the maintenance of public worship; (c) the cost of heating, lighting and cleaning Church and Halls; (d) rates, taxes, and insurance on heritable property (including the Manse); (e) the maintenance of an adequate Fabric Fund; and (f) salaries of Church Officer, Organist, *etc.*

The Board carried responsibility too for seeing that the property was maintained in good order and adequately covered by insurance. Any credit outstanding at the close of the financial year was to be applied for 'general purposes', which were defined as including supplement to stipend, addition to Fabric Fund and the creation of reserve funds for property or for further endowment of stipend.

In 1962 the General Assembly appointed a Special Committee to consider whether it was desirable that there should be one standard method of administering the affairs of congregations, if so what form such constitution should take, and how the change-over should be effected. In its first report the Committee came up with the interesting information that at that date 417 congregations worked on the *quoad sacra* basis, 232 had a Deacons' Court, 127 had a Board of Management, and 579 operated under the Model Deed. The Committee after due consideration had come to the position that while from many points of view it would be desirable to have consistency in this field, it would be unwise to push through legislation to compel the adoption of any one type. In a later report of 1965 they submitted an amended Model Deed and the following year the Assembly 'recommended and urged those congregations which had not already done so to adopt the Model Deed in its amended form'. This in fact a considerable number did.

Of the changes effected in the Deed many were fairly trivial and by way of tidying up, but two were quite significant. For one thing the procedure to be followed in the adoption of the Model Deed was simplified and in particular it was no longer necessary to transfer the heritable property into the name of the General Trustees.

One of the objections always advanced, especially by former Free Church congregations, against the Model Deed was that where there was a large Kirk Session the choice was either that a more or less equal number of elected members produced a body of quite unmanageable proportions (150 or more); or else if the number were kept down to a token of say nine or ten the Board was difficult to distinguish from the Session. To meet this difficulty provision is made whereby a congregation may resolve on a two thirds majority that it will have a small Congregational Board, say 19, of which ten will be Elders nominated by the Session and nine members of the congregation elected at the Stated Annual Meeting.

It is unfortunate that with all the thought given to the Model Deed it has not yet proved possible to come up with a simple name for the 'Congregational Boarder'!

In this day and age when it is the congregational members who foot all the bills and thereby make the existence of the congregation possible, it is right that the financial affairs should be in the hands of a body answerable to the congregation and the Model Deed guarantees this right.

24
WHAT IS
THE COLLECTION?

TALK of alms dishes and of the offertory is not infrequently heard in our Churches today, but to the good old dyed-in-the-wool Scottish Churchman it is still 'the plate' and it exists for the in-gathering of 'the collection'. Increasingly the uplifting of the offering is coming to be seen as an integral part of worship – 'Let us worship God in our offering' – and the givings of the people as part of a stewardship that concerns more than just worldly goods. But it has not always been so.

In thinking of the collection it is well to remember that in the early days in Scotland there was no call for the parishioners to subscribe for the maintenance of Church property or for stipend, for the law laid that duty on the heritors.

But one burden which the Scots Kirk loyally accepted from the start was the support of the poor and accordingly it was for this that collections were regularly taken.

An interesting entry in an Ayrshire Kirk Session minute book consists in an appeal to the heritors to have the kirkyard dykes repaired so that there might be 'but ane entry into the churchyard at which two Elders may attend to receive the contributions of the people every Sabbath morning'. The minute goes on with disarming frankness to explain that 'the disadvantage of having two or three entries into the churchyard must be obvious to every person as occasioning loss to the poor'.

It is recorded that in one rural parish where 'the lafts' were reached by outside stairs, ladles were substituted for bags for taking the collection in these upper regions. The advantage was that these could be handed down in full view of the congregation so that Elders concerned were not needlessly 'led into temptation'!

Ordinary and Special

The emergence from 1740 onwards of the independent denominations created an entirely new situation, for here you had congregations that strictly had no responsibility for the poor (except within their own ranks), but which had to find money for ordinary running expenses, fabric, stipend, *etc.* The vast number of Free Church congregations that appeared after 1843, and the not inconsiderable number of *quoad sacra* parishes erected around the same period, likewise faced the need of raising large sums for their own day-to-day outlays.

It was about that same time that the Kirk in Scotland experienced a growing awareness of its call to a wider service in Foreign Mission and other forms of activity and witness. So that the support of the poor came to be but one of the extramural commitments. It was this which led to the practice of dividing collections into 'ordinary' and 'special'.

The collection taken on entering, or by bag, plate or ladle in course of the service, was recognised as the ordinary collection, designed to meet domestic needs. From time to time special collections were uplifted for special non-congregational objects. These might be gathered in course of the service, but more often they were taken on leaving and so were called 'retiring collections'. It was the great John White who complained that too often they were 'very retiring'.

As the special objects grew in number, and as the insistence of the various committees to be remembered increased in intensity, the Assembly, with a view to regulating matters to some extent, passed an Act each year appointing those Sundays when special collections were to be taken and fixing the Scheme to which each was to be devoted. This system suffered from two obvious defects. First, it took no account of the vastly differing scale of activity and financial need of one Scheme against another; and second, the annual income from the whole Church for a particular object might be halved because its collection fell on a day of disastrously bad weather throughout the country.

Ourselves and Others

As the number of fields in which the Kirk was becoming active increased and the number of appeals grew to embarrassing, if not alarming, proportions, the Weekly Freewill Offering (WFO) Scheme came to be widely adopted. Under this the member undertook a certain weekly rate of giving for all Church purposes, and the responsible court of the congregation said they would ensure that members were relieved of special appeals of every sort. In its original conception the WFO scheme provided that as well as promising a weekly sum the member indicated how much of this was for 'Ourselves' and how much for 'Others'. In this way the member was given the chance to contribute separately – if in one envelope – for both domestic and wider needs of the Church, and the injunction of the Assembly was being honoured in that each member was being given the opportunity of subscribing to each and all of the Schemes.

To assist financial boards in making allocations of the sums received, the Assembly each year issued a standard division of £1 among all the Schemes based on the proportion of the amounts spent by the various Committees during the previous year.

In theory this seemed a foolproof system, but it too broke down, partly because more and more members were not indicating a division between Ourselves and Others, and partly because some of those who did so divide did not put into the envelope the amount required to carry out the division. From here it was but a step to the point where financial boards sent up for the Schemes of the Church what was left over after all the local bills had been paid – a practice giving more satisfaction at the local level than in Edinburgh.

Towards a New System

The position outlined above represented a far cry from the old idea that every member must at least be given opportunity to contribute to each and every scheme – and, presumably, to withhold from any Scheme of which the contributor did not approve. It led to a period during which various of the Committees concerned – more venturesome, or more desperate (or less honest) than others – were approaching congregations and even individual members directly and pushing their claims through 'partner plans' and 'targets' and 'house collecting boxes' and 'bonds of covenant'. And in the end it led to the emergence of the Co-ordinated Appeal which in turn led to the Co-ordinated Budget and Allocation.

In most congregations nowadays there is but one collection, taken normally during the service and consisting mainly of envelopes, and from the income which it provides all the domestic needs of the congregation, as well as its share for the support of the wider work of the Church, have to be met.

25
WHAT WERE SEAT RENTS?

IN most churches of any age, you will still today find at the end of the bookboard in each pew a little brass frame designed to hold a card. The card will probably say how welcome you are to sit there or something equally innocuous. Had you visited the Church half a century ago the card would have shown a pew number followed by some such legend as 'Six sittings at 7/6 per half year' followed by the names of the paid-up seat-holders. The amount of the rents varied as between one part of the 'house' and another – even as in the theatre. This was a survival from the day when seat-rents were an important item in the economy of the average congregation, that in turn being a carry-over from an earlier time when, unless you could claim to be one of the 'poor', you could actually be prevented from occupying a seat in the parish church unless you had rented it – and duly paid the rent.

As explained elsewhere, the heritors who had the duty of building and maintaining the churches had a right to sittings therein. True they had to reserve free of charge a number of sittings for the poor – the 'Paupers' Pews', a title hardly likely to attract occupants. But thereafter they could let sittings with a view of reimbursing themselves against certain outlays. Hence the seat rents.

When independent congregations began to appear, and especially when *quoad sacra* charges came to be erected, seat rents appealed as providing a steady and reliable source of income. A case is recorded where the Minister would baptise only the children of seat-holders. In this way a minimum fee of a half-year's seat rent was obtained for the service, but it seemed an odd way of judging the Christian commitment of the parents.

Let by Public Auction

In 1819 an advertisement appeared in the Glasgow press 'respectfully informing' the public of the opening of a New Seceding Meeting-House in Regent Place and giving dates and times when 'those desirous of obtaining property therein' might have the opportunity of choosing for themselves where they wanted to sit, after which sittings were to be available to such as might apply.

A very serious situation developed in 1798 in the Parish of Neilston when the heritors decided to let the sittings to the highest bidders at a public auction within the church itself. They had extended the building the year before, but it was still inadequate to meet the needs of a parish that was relentlessly expanding, including as it did the growing town of Barrhead. From the heritors' point of view the auction proved a great success, seats fetching as much as 31/6 (average 12/4) in a day when a worker in one of the local mills was earning 16/- a week. In face of much muttering and grumbling the practice continued until 1826, a year of particularly bad trade and widespread unemployment. The good folk of Neilston decided not to bid for their seats but just to come and occupy them as usual.

To this open declaration of war the heritors were quick to respond with an interdict from the Sheriff against 'all and sundry' from entering the seats of the church without the heritors' authority. Alexander Fleming, the Parish Minister, was not a man to be cowed by such a display of force, particularly as he had himself been carrying on a large-scale campaign against the heritors for some time. If his people were to be kept out, he would stay out with them. He had a pulpit of sorts erected against the outside wall and for the next eight years, summer and winter, he preached there – yes, for eight long years.

Insiders and Outsiders

Quite a number of people were continuing to pay for their sittings and resented having to part with good money to sit inside when if they wished to worship they had to brave the elements and stand outside. So an action was raised in the church courts to require Mr Fleming to conduct services inside the building. In its own slow and stately fashion the process passed through Presbytery and Synod and reached the General Assembly which in 1829 passed an Act (no less) ordering Mr Fleming back into the church 'to give sermon'.

Replied Mr Fleming, 'The Assembly says I must preach inside, but not that I may not preach outside; so I'll do both'. So began a programme that was to continue for five years – every Sunday morning a service attended by heritors, their tenants, and other seat-holders was held in church; in the afternoon a service attended by mill-workers and others, without sittings or money to pay for them, was held in the kirkyard.

Meantime another case affecting the good Mr Fleming was making its stately progress through the civil courts. He was demanding that the heritors build a new church adequate for the growing population while they for their part were determined that repairs and extensions to the existing building would meet the case. With this in view they wanted to carry out a survey, but he refused them access. They had duplicate keys made and went forward with their survey. He charged them with breaking and entering.

Indecency and Illegality

In the Court of Session Mr Fleming lost his case for a new building, costs being awarded against him. Support, however, was coming from unexpected quarters and he was encouraged to go on to the House of Lords. Here again he lost, but in the course of his judgement the Lord Chancellor had some very pungent things to say about the practice of letting sittings for rent in the landward parishes, referring in particular to the 'indecency and illegality' of holding the auction within the sacred building itself.

Under cover of this, the Minister and his flock of 'outsiders' returned to the church, taking possession of their former sittings without offering to pay any rent. For their part the heritors were probably sufficiently relieved at not being required to build a new church that they let the matter go. And one cannot but believe that after eight years of preaching in the open air, even so bonnie a fechter as Alexander Fleming was glad to return to the shelter of his pulpit.

The
MINISTRY

WHAT is a Minister? A good question, as the Ministry of National Insurance discovered long ago when they decided to regard Ministers as self-employed persons. They were trying to solve a problem of classification for their own purposes and also trying to pacify Ministers who bitterly resented being described as 'employed' – which seemed to imply a master-servant relationship quite foreign to the nature of their office. Under today's NI regulations, and for the purposes thereof, Ministers are seen as 'employed persons'.

The relationship of a Minister of the National Church with his Parish is a unique affair. He is not engaged and appointed, he is called and inducted; he is not paid a salary, he is in receipt of a stipend; he cannot be dismissed by the body that called, but only by the Presbytery that inducted him, and then only for moral delinquency. To be quite correct the ministry is a *munus publicus,* an appointment involving duties to the public, a position shared with, for example, judges of the realm.

26
WHAT IS A
SELECTION SCHOOL?

IT is universally accepted that the Ministry is more than just an occupation, or even a profession – it is a calling. From which it follows that the aspirant for the ministry requires more than merely the appropriate academic training – he must have an inner sense of dedication, must see himself as one chosen by God and called by Him to this form of service. While this sense of call is essential, it is not by itself a guarantee of the successful discharge of a ministry. For that demands an understanding of people, a facility for responding in an appropriate way – which will vary from one case to the next – to those who come seeking help. It is a kind of ability which experience can foster, but which if it isn't there in the first place is not easy to instill.

It was all put rather neatly (can anyone tell me by whom?) in the remark that the requirements for the ministry are summed up in 'the three G's' – Greek, Grace and Gumption. If you haven't any Greek you can go to a University and learn some; if you are short on grace you can get down on your knees and pray for some; but if you haven't any gumption you'd be well advised to give up all thought of the parish ministry right now!

Nomination by Presbytery

It has always been required that to enter upon a Divinity course with a view to the ministry the aspirant must first secure nomination by the Presbytery within whose bounds he resides. The duty of the Presbytery was laid down in the last century – it has 'to satisfy itself by careful enquiry of his moral and religious character. He must produce a certificate, given on sufficient grounds by the Moderator of the Kirk Session of the parish within which he resides that he is in communion with the church and that his character and deportment are suitable to his views'. The Basis and Plan of Union of 1929 requires *inter alia*:

> Before entering on the study of Divinity in any of the Theological Faculties, candidates for the Ministry of

> the Church must satisfy the Presbytery with which
> they are connected of their character, and the motives
> which have actuated them to seek entrance into the
> work of the Ministry. They must further produce
> certificates showing that they are in full communion
> with the Church, and be nominated by their Pres-
> byteries for admission as candidates for the ministry.

Candidates have still today to be nominated by their Presbyteries, but there is wide diversity in the steps taken to test suitability. In most cases a letter from the candidate's minister, followed by an interview by a committee, is the practice followed. The Minister has probably gone on the fact that the person is a member, a regular worshipper, a Sunday School teacher, a member of the choir. In every case the testing is directed towards the element of grace and not to the 'gumption' element which would be difficult to sustain in any case.

The Selection School

In 1967 the Committee on Education for the Ministry reported to the Assembly that they had been looking very closely into more efficient ways of screening candidates for the Ministry, 'the notion rampant in certain circles that anyone who offers himself to become a Minister of the Church of Scotland must be destroyed'. They had held a 'pilot' Selection School in St Andrews the previous December when ten candidates, split into two groups of five, had been invited to attend. The school lasted from just after lunch one day until tea-time the next and each candi-date was interviewed three times by the Director and two of his Assessors as well as by a trained psychologist. The candidates took part in an informal discussion group and also in conducting a committee meeting. There was, too, a written section which involved a General Information

Test as well as the composition of a 'tactful letter'.

On the basis of the experiment the committee was unanimous in recommending the adoption of some such scheme for the sifting of candidates. The following year it was reported that five further schools had been held, the length of the session having been extended to two full days and the method followed being an adaptation of that used by the Civil Service Selection Board. The Committee was fully satisfied that a step forward in the right direction had been taken.

If on the strength of appearance and performance at the school the candidate is recommended by the Selection Board, then it is open to the Presbytery to nominate him. If, however, the Board is not satisfied the candidate is told of this and also of the fact that he or she is at liberty to return to a second school, and even to a third, at intervals of normally not less than twelve months, and involving different Assessors who have no access to the records of previous appearances. A fourth chance may even be granted, but this only on petition to the full Committee. There is also machinery for appealing where a candidate feels he has had less than a fair testing, or even if he wants to plead that special circumstances had militated against his performance.

Recognising how shattered the candidate may be on being turned down for a task to which he feels convinced in the depths of his heart that God is calling him, a counsellor is appointed in each case to seek to help the individual through what may be a very trying experience.

Does it work?

It has to be said that there has been in some quarters a certain suspicion of, and hostility towards, the Selection School. Some say it does nothing to solve the problem, nor can it be denied that the complete misfit is still a feature of the scene.

A difficulty can arise from the fact that while the Kirk is in full command in choosing candidates for the ministry, she has no control over who may enrol at the University for a course in divinity. A turned-down candidate, hoping for better luck next year, enters for his first University course, which is passed with distinction. Thus at the end of the course the candidate has a BD with Distinction but is not accepted for the Ministry. Admirable material for an Assembly speech! We lament the shortage of ministers, yet here is a brilliant student dying to offer his services but the Board doesn't want to know him. It can all be made to sound damning. Yet the fact remains that academic brilliance does not of itself make a good minister – as the cynic says, many a congregation has been killed by degrees.

So long as the successful discharge of the various duties of the ministry demands more than just Greek and grace, it is important we should early be able to discover those who lack that something more – for their own sake no less than for the Kirk's. The Selection School is clearly not the complete answer, even if it is the nearest thing to an answer we have so far discovered.

27
WHAT IS A
VACANCY COMMITTEE?

WHEN, through the death, demission or departure of its Minister, a charge falls vacant the first question to arise is that of reappraisal – formerly called readjustment – determining the future of the cause. Let it be this has been resolved in the congregation's favour – *ie* they have been given what used to be called the *congé d'élire*, the right to choose and call a Minister. Then the first step to be taken once the Roll has been made up is to elect a Vacancy Committee. This is a body varying in size according to the membership-roll, consisting of members whose names appear on the Electoral Register, representative as far as possible of all aspects of the congregation's life, and it is their task to bring forward the names of one or more persons thought suitable for appointment as next minister of the charge.

It is for the Committee itself at its first meeting to elect a Convener and a Vice-Convener. The interim moderator may be invited (and if so should certainly agree) to accept the Convenership. In any case he should certainly act as Assessor, always on hand to give general advice. A Secretary is also appointed who need not be a member though there is obvious advantage if he or she is. Minutes of all meetings are carefully kept. The doings of the Committee are strictly confidential, every effort being made to ensure that they are kept so.

Difficulties

The task confronting the members of the Committee is a formidable one, added to which they start off with two distinct disadvantages. The first is generally a complete lack of experience in the field. For most congregations a vacancy is a relatively rare thing – in some cases not a single member of the Committee has a clear recollection of the previous vacancy let alone any experience of it. So, for most of the Committee at least, they are moving into virgin territory, and doing so in a rather nervous frame of mind.

The other disadvantage is that so many of the members take their responsibility so desperately seriously. It is a fact, of course, that choosing the right person for Minister can be a critical factor in the life of any congregation and members of the Vacancy Committee seem often to be terrified at the gravity of the duty thrust upon them. It is this which explains the extravagant senseless and insensitive way in which they can sometimes go about their task. A little more faith in divine guidance and a little conviction that it is not all resting on their weak and unsupported shoulders, would prove of great help. At the opposite extreme, of course, are the over-confident.

Narrowing the Choice

Recent legislation provides that for each vacancy the Presbytery has to appoint a small Advisory Committee which meets first with the Kirk Session and then with the Committee to discuss the kind of Ministry that would be best suited to the particular demands of this charge. The members of the Vacancy Committee will of course have their own ideas on this subject and they are not bound in any way by the views of the conferring body.

In this context it can be amusing to note how often in the end of the day the nominee selected bears no remote resemblance to the identikit portrait so studiously and laboriously prepared at this early stage. It having been resolved that they want a male, married, with experience in a first charge, between the ages of 35 and 45, the sole nominee duly appears – an unmarried girl of 28 straight from college. The sage who opined there is nowt stranger than fowk had maybe been a member of a Vacancy Committee.

Reaching a Decision

By this stage the Committee is ready to go into action. They may decide to advertise their vacancy, inviting applications from interested parties. On the other hand some dislike the idea of candidature, feeling it is out of keeping with the idea of a 'call'. Generally, however, they will be prepared to receive suggestions – from whatever source. In one way or another the Committee gets a list which they prune, first of all by eliminating those who on the face of things seem quite unsuitable. They then begin the business of hearing candidates. The members form themselves into small groups (size determined by the capacity of cars available), and visit the charge of the person in whom they are interested, to hear him (or her) on his own ground. There he is assessed, in however rough-and-ready a way, on how effective his present ministry is proving. Every attempt should be made to do this kind of thing in as quiet and discreet a fashion as possible, bearing in mind the relation of the Minister concerned to his own people. Five eager worshippers disembarking at the main door with an enquiry whether there are special seats for visitors is not recommended.

Out of all this extensive touring there generally emerge the names of one or two 'likelies', the usual drill being for these to be heard on common ground and interviewed by the entire committee so that from among them a sole nominee may be chosen. Some thought should be given in advance to the kind of questions to be asked, keeping in mind that this is an interview and not an inquisition. Should there be great difficulty in deciding between two finalists the Committee is usually wise to drop both and start afresh. A serious division in the Committee is sure to be reflected in the voting of the congregation and it is in nobody's interest to have a sole nominee turn down the appointment because of the half-hearted signing of the Call.

The End of the Road

Once the stage has been reached of finding a sole nominee and having his acceptance, or of proposing a leet to be heard and voted on by the entire congregation (though this is not to be recommended), the Committee has completed its task and bows off the stage. Arranging for the candidate to be heard and for an election to be held is purely Kirk Session business, while the subsequent induction lies within the domain of the Presbytery. It is not unusual for the Vacancy Committee to end its days as a Tea and Buns Committee responsible for the Welcome Social, the inevitable follow-on to the Induction Service. Then, like the old soldier of the legend, the Vacancy Committee just fades away.

It is unfortunate there is no opportunity for the Committee to be officially discharged, for then occasion might be taken to record the gratitude of the congregation for an always diffi-cult and responsible – and often quite arduous – duty faithfully performed. In most cases, certainly, the Vacancy Committee fully deserves it.

28

WHAT IS A CALL?

THERE are two separate and distinct senses in which the word 'call' is used in the ministry, and it is important at the outset to distinguish clearly between them. When we speak of a man (or a woman) having a call to the ministry, we mean that this is for him no mere job, he has a sense of vocation, he feels chosen of God to do this thing; when we speak of Mr Smith having received a call to the Parish of Invermuchty we mean there has been put into his hands a formal paper signed by the people of that parish inviting him to come and be their Minister. It is with this latter sense of the term that we are here concerned.

The magnificent language and lofty senti-ments of this paper are worth putting on record. It explains that the undersigned –

> … *desirous of promoting the glory of God and the good of the Church, being destitute of a fixed pastor*

and being assured, by good information and our own experience, of the ministerial ability, piety, and prudence, as also of the suitableness to our capacities of the gifts of you, Mr John Smith, Minister of the Gospel, have agreed to invite, call and entreat, like as we by these presents do heartily invite, call and entreat, you to undertake the office of Pastor among us, and the charge of our souls; and further, upon your accepting this our Call, promise you all dutiful respect, encouragement and obedience in the Lord, and we promise to contribute heartily, as the Lord shall enable us, towards the maintenance of the Christian ministry and the furtherance of the Gospel: In witness whereof ...

Needless to say, a Committee is busy devising a new and simpler form of words.

Why sign a Call?

In early days five or six candidates would regularly be invited to occupy the pulpit of a vacant charge and an election, either by ballot or by open vote, would thereafter be held. The Call had a very significant place in this set-up, providing as it did the opportunity for the member whose candidate had been defeated to indicate that he was happy to accept the decision of the majority and that he would give the successful candidate his unstinted support.

Nowadays with the preaching competition happily a thing of the past, and the voting being simply For or Against the election of the sole nominee, there are those who say that the Call is simply a duplication. If there has been a good turn-out of voters and the nominee has been elected unanimously by these, what is the point in resurrecting all this archaic language merely for the sake of presenting him with a sheaf of papers? A possible answer is that for the Minister concerned it can be a worthwhile experience in a later year to resurrect the Call and see how it compares with the actual support received.

Origin of the Call

According to the Assembly of 1782 the Call is 'the immemorial and constitutional practice of the Church'. It has far too long and interesting a history to be lightly discarded, even if it has lost much of its original significance.

It is said that the practice of giving a Call dates from 1649, shortly after the overthrow of Episcopacy, and it is certain that it existed in 1690 when it was ratified by an Act of Assembly. It represented a formal declaration on the part of the congregation concerned of their desire to have the person named as their Minister and a promise to give him all due honour and support. One thing that was not clear at this time, that was to lead to a vast deal of trouble, was who had the right to sign. Was a Call subscribed by Heritors and Elders adequate, or had it also to bear the names of the male heads of families? They never got round to imagining that individual members might sign. Or women.

Patronage

The operation of patronage became a matter of acute concern when an Act was passed by Parliament in 1712 restoring the principle. This was destined to have a profound influence on the history of the Kirk which it continuously and sorely disturbed until its final repeal in 1874. Patronage had its roots in pre-Reformation times when a man of substance would make grants of land to the Church for the creation of a benefice but would retain the right of appointment thereto. By the Revolution Settlement of 1690 the right of presentation was vested in the Heritors and Elders of the Parish. When patronage was restored in 1712 the Jacobite party saw their opportunity, for they could now fill parishes with men of known prelatic sympathies. But although the Act was passed and patronage was back the people were to have the right of objecting to the person presented. In place of a positive right to Call there had been substituted a negative right to object – but not to veto.

Secession and Disruption

There was laid before the Assembly of 1731 an Overture proposing that when the filling of a vacant charge fell to the Presbytery (as not infrequently happened because the patron declined or deliberately delayed exercising his right), the appointment was to be made upon a Call from the Heritors and Elders alone. The person so called was then to be proposed to the congregation who were given the right of objecting for good and adequate reason – clearly a return to the Revolution Settlement position. The following year this was passed into an Act, against which Ebenezer Erskine, Minister at Stirling, declaimed in a famous sermon, thus triggering off a train of events that led to the First Secession.

The Ten Years' Conflict that culminated in the Disruption began in 1833 when the Assembly passed the Veto Act ordaining that when dealing with a Call to a vacant parish, if less than half of the male heads of families had appended their names, the Presbytery was bound to refuse to induct. The details of that story can be found on page 142. Suffice it here to say that through that whole period from 1732 till 1843 the Kirk was torn in conflict over some question relating to the Call. South of the border they were fighting about franchise, rotten boroughs and what-have-you; but in Scotland the battle of democracy was fought on Church territory over the question of the right to call a Minister.

Sometimes today an impatient member of a Vacancy Committee, anxious to 'get on with the job', will refer to the Call as 'just another piece of red tape'. The response could be given, 'Red, yes, for it is stained with the blood of your fathers'.

29
WHAT IS AN INDUCTION?

Notice is hereby given to all concerned, that if they, or any of them, have anything to object to in the life or doctrine of the said Mr John Bloggs they may repair to the Presbytery which is to meet at ...... with certification that if no relevant objection be then made and immediately substantiated, the Presbytery will proceed without further delay.

SO concludes the edict which is solemnly served on a vacant congregation on the two Sundays preceding the day of the induction of their new minister. The edict had begun by narrating the fact that the said Mr John Bloggs had been duly elected, that his Call had been sustained by the Presbytery, that his translation had been agreed by the releasing Presbytery, and that it had been resolved that the Presbytery should meet at the Church of the vacant parish on the day appointed for his admission.

What is this induction about which so much is made? In these days of streamlining it would be much simpler if the new Minister came along and took up his duties on a date agreed as any other professional man would do, without all this fuss. Should the congregation want to hold a welcome social that would be up to them, but the Presbytery would not need to meet as well.

Legal Significance

'Induction' is a comparatively modern term, the

word originally used being 'admission', and this was comparable to investment. It used to be that land was transmitted by the symbolic delivery, in the presence of witnesses, of *sasines,* for instance earth and stones for land, a clap and hammer for a mill, a net for a salmon-fishing. In like manner the new Minister was actually carried in to the church and installed in the pulpit, thereby taking 'actual, real and corporate possession' of teind, manse, and kirklands. Induction therefore is the public symbol of the Minister having entered into the rights and privileges as well as into the duties and obligations of his charge.

It was also particularly important under the system of patronage, for in the formalities of induction lay the Church's opportunity to screen the men being presented to her livings. The Kirk could not tell the patron whom he was to present, but she could say whether the person proposed to be presented was properly qualified. Otherwise, no induction.

Today when the sources of stipend lie wholly within the Kirk's control, when manses and glebes are vested in Church trustees, this special importance no longer attaches to induction, but it still has a legal significance in that it constitutes a bond between Minister and congregation which cannot in any circumstances be severed by the latter and by the former only with consent of Presbytery. Induction is still officially *ad vitam aut culpam* (for life or till fault), which means that the Minister cannot be ousted unless he has been guilty of some grave fault. This nowadays is taken to mean some serious moral delinquency, or having reached the age of 65, and not just that he is unsuited for the ministry or that he does not fit well into this particular charge. It has to be admitted that unsuitability can often do more harm than moral fault, and during the days of disputed settlements it was not uncommon for a man to be deprived from his charge on the ground that he was 'unfit and unmeet to edify', nor is it impossible that such a charge would still be competent. It is doubtful, though, if any Church court would be prepared to raise such an action much less to convict under it.

For the Congregation

For the congregation no less than for the Minister, the act of induction has real meaning. As has been said, the parishioners are given the opportunity at a meeting of Presbytery before the actual service of induction to object to the new Minister. It should be noted that it is only on grounds of life or doctrine that objection may competently be taken – that is to say, it must be shown that the person concerned is unfit for the ministry, not just unfitted to minister to this parish.

Attention is sometimes drawn to the fact that it is only after the Minister has been inducted that a question is put to the congregation regarding their acceptance of him as their Minister. What, it is asked, would the Presbytery do were the congregation to say 'No'? The answer is that this question does not have to do with the acceptance of the Minister – he has already been chosen by popular vote and ample opportunity provided for the lodging of objections – it has to do wholly with the spirit of dedication and consecration in which the members face the future with their new Minister. He has renewed his vows – it is fitting they be given an opportunity to renew theirs.

For the Presbytery

The service of induction has its significance too for the Presbytery. It is a reminder of the important Presbyterian principle that the Minister is not the employee of the congregation to be engaged by them and to begin his duties on a day mutually agreeable. The Minister is the executive of the Presbytery, and he calls no man Master save Jesus Christ.

It is good too for the Presbytery to visit its various congregations and for its members to be reminded of their corporate responsibility. It is so easy, especially in these days of continuous heavy demands, for a Minister to find his horizons bounded by the limits of his own parish and his own problems. It is good for him to be reminded that he has brother Ministers from whom he may gain – and to whom he may give – encouragement, advice, and help.

If with the passing of the years the Induction Service has lost something of its legal significance, it has lost nothing of its spiritual importance. All that it means is surely beautifully summarised in the words of the Induction prayer:

> *Visit, we beseech Thee, this people with Thy love and favour, and bless the ministry now begun to their spiritual nourishment and growth in grace. Grant that they may be enlightened and edified by the preaching of the Word, quickened by Thy Spirit, sustained by Thy sacraments, established in all holy living, and kept by Thy power through faith unto salvation.*

30
WHAT IS AN APPOINTMENT AD VITAM AUT CULPAM?

THE appointment of a minister, inducted by the Presbytery to the charge of a Church and Parish is said to be *ad vitam aut culpam* – for life or until fault. Such a Minister cannot be dismissed by the congregation in any circumstances, and can be dismissed by the Presbytery – or by the General Assembly for that matter – only after some serious fault in life or doctrine has been confessed or has been found proven after due trial. As explained later there are circumstances in which the pastoral tie may nowadays be 'dissolved'.

Appointment *ad vitam aut culpam* is a most unusual state of affairs whose conditions are presumed to apply to judges, sheriffs, University professors, and Ministers of the Church of Scotland all of whom are regarded as holding a *munus publicus*, *ie* an office involving duties to the public. Other offices may carry such terms of appointment, but the presumption is always against it.

Trial by Libel

The only way in former days in which a Minister could be got out of his parish was by being deposed from the ministry. He had to be charged with some grave fault, and, unless he confessed, his guilt had to be proved by full process of law. If found guilty he would almost certainly be deposed from the ministry – 'unfrocked' as the popular phrase had it. Short of that there was no way in which his ministry in a particular parish could be terminated. The legal process by which his case was dealt with was called trial by libel, the word 'libel' referring to the formal indictment which with great precision and particularity charged a Minister or Probationer with misconduct or heresy.

Trial by libel is today very rare indeed. In fact at the level of Assembly such cases would not now be heard. In 1961 legislation was introduced setting up a Judicial Commission to conduct the trial in any case where a libel judgment has been made the subject of appeal to the supreme court.

Congregation in an Unsatisfactory State

Over the past thirty-odd years, changes have occurred which have had the effect of whittling away what was once the impregnable position occupied by the Minister inducted *ad vitam aut culpam*. Let us glance at these.

As said, the form of trial by libel is today little more than a memory − a vague one at that. Whether the conduct of ministers has improved or the censoriousness of Presbyteries has diminished, one would hesitate to say. It is possible that the process is so difficult and complicated that courts are reluctant to embark upon it.

In any case a new process was introduced in 1960 whereby it has become possible to dissolve the pastoral tie binding a Minister to a particular charge without deposing him from the ministry. This is contained in the Act anent Congregations in an Unsatisfactory State, and provides that a Presbytery, after due investigation and attempt at rectification, if satisfied (a) that the congregation is in an unsatisfactory state, and (b) that this is wholly or mainly due to faults personal to the Minister, may proceed to sever the tie created at his induction. The Church takes steps to ensure that what it considers adequate provision is made for the Minister in such a case.

The Act also creates machinery for appeal, which does not go direct to the Assembly but to the Judicial Commission to hear evidence and reach a judgment upon the facts. This is reported to the Assembly which is to ratify the judgment of the Commission and go on to say what is to happen. This cannot be seen as a sentence since fault in the sense of *culpa* is not involved.

There were obvious weaknesses in the Act, particularly the need to show that the blame for the disastrous situation in the congregation lies squarely at the Minister's door. Trouble in a congregation will be allowed to build up for a long time before it is brought to the attention of the Presbytery, and by then it will be true to say that, no matter who started the mischief, by now quite a few will have contributed towards it.

An amending Act was passed in 1988 which

required that it be proved: (a) the congregation is in an unsatisfactory state; and (b) that state will continue until the pastoral tie is dissolved. The Act also outlines a very elaborate procedure to be followed. It is early days to say how satisfactorily the new arrangements will work. For our present purpose it will suffice to show this as a breach of the *ad vitam aut culpam* system of tenure.

Age Limit

The year 1972 saw a new Act passed providing that the fact of a Minister having passed his seventieth birthday was automatically to put him in the position of having retired from the charge on that date. He might continue to serve in the charge after his seventieth birthday, but would do so on a *de die in diem* basis. '*Vita*' has acquired an age-limit. Act IV 1995 lowered the compulsory retiral age to 65. Neither of these regulations has any effect on the rights of 'sitting' Ministers.

Congregations in Changed Circumstances

The Assembly in 1974 passed an Act whereby when the circumstances of a congregation have dramatically changed – as can so easily happen in an area of urban development today – although nobody has been at fault in any sense at all, the Presbytery can step in and dissolve the pastoral tie, having made satisfactory arrangements for the future of both Minister and people concerned. I am not aware of any case where advantage has been taken of the provisions of this Act.

Security of Tenure

The really important thing to be secured for the ministry is that a man set to speak for God among a people should not be dependent for the security of his position on his ability to win popularity among them. The situation may well arise where the man commissioned to lead his people in holy things finds that his duty requires him to adopt a line which, for the time being at least, is unpopular and could well lead to his being 'given his books'. That situation must never be allowed to arise within the Church.

On the other hand the Minister has to realise that although it has been put out of the power of his congregation to dismiss him, no matter how much he 'annoys' them, there is no particular virtue in unpopularity for its own sake, and that having his congregation in a state of perpetual discord and unrest is no proof that he is conducting a ministry approved in the sight of God.

31

WHAT WAS VICTUAL STIPEND?

ANY question regarding stipend in the Church of Scotland brings us immediately into contact with the Committee on the Maintenance of the Ministry. One can do no better than quote the opening words of Dr A J H Gibson's interesting work, *Stipend in the Church of Scotland*:

> *The General Assembly have entrusted stipend in the Church of Scotland in all its aspects to a standing committee named the Committee on the Maintenance of the Ministry. This Committee does its work through a Fund with the stately title 'The Fund for the Maintenance of the Ministry', which is an abbreviation of the 'Fund for the Maintenance of Gospel Ordinances for the People in every Parish in Scotland through a Territorial Ministry'.*

It is regrettable that the popular 'M of M' conveys the impression that the fund exists to maintain Ministers. In fact its object is to maintain Gospel ordinances in every parish throughout the land.

Stipend, Gibson claims, derives from the oldest fund in the world, 'the tithe'. In Scotland the basic provision for the ministry is standardised stipend which is the up-to-date version of the teind, and this in turn is just the tenth called for by Moses to maintain Priests and Levites. This tenth was not the brainchild of Moses who was merely regularising a principle accepted from very ancient times. While, however, we may thus trace back into antiquity the roots of stipend, we have to recognise that both the concept and the character of the provision have changed much with the passing of the centuries.

For the purpose of the present Answer, we must content ourselves with a glance at the history of stipend as it existed in the Kirk prior to the Union of 1929. In the next Answer (32) something is said about the provision made in other branches of the Church in Scotland, and a word is added about the position today.

Standardisation of Stipend

The Church of Scotland (Property and Endowments) Act 1925 made a most important provision in regard to stipend – that in respect of every parish in Scotland the burden of teind was to be fixed for all time coming as a definite annual sum of money. What had been a fluctuating sum was to become a standard charge. It also provided for the wiping out of trivial amounts and the redemption of modest sums. The basis of calculation was to be the average amount of stipend for the past fifty years leading up to 1922 with an addition of five per cent, and the change was to be made at latest on the first vacancy occurring. A Minister could elect to standardise, and this had the effect of creating a vacancy for purposes of the Act. This was standardisation and today it has been effected in every parish in the land.

For more than a century prior to this the

matter of stipend in the old parishes had been regulated by an Act of 1808 which required that stipend be paid in money and not in victual (actual bags of grain) as had previously been the custom, and which set forth the basis upon which the valuation was to be carried out. The teind was a tax not on the land but on the fruits of the land (hence its expression in victual) and it had been fixed always in terms of grain − so many bolls of barley, so many firkins of meal, so many chalders of bear, and so on.

Another peculiarity was that stipend vested in the incumbent and did so in equal installments at Whitsunday and Michaelmas − after the crop had been sown and when it was reaped. This meant that whoever was actually Minister of the Parish on 15th May and 29th September acquired the right to a half-year's stipend irrespective of how long he had been there or how long he was to stay there. Blood-curdling tales are told of dying Ministers kept alive by artificial respiration till the dawn of term day. It is worth noting that Michaelmas not Martinmas was the deciding date and that although exactly half of the stipend vested at these times the division of the year was into 'halves' of a quite unequal kind.

Fiars' Prices

Had a Minister wanted to go around with a horse and cart collecting his 'victual' he could probably have done so immediately the harvest was in; but when it had to be calculated in terms of cash it was essential to await the crop being sold to determine its monetary value. In each county early in March the Sheriff sat with a jury of 15 to hear evidence regarding the prices that had been ruling for the various kinds of grain in that area throughout the winter. This was called the Fiars' Court, and the result of its deliberations was the fixing of the Fiars' Prices. These provided the yardstick by which all ministers in the county would be able to calculate the amount due to them from the various heritors within their parishes. The figures are set forth in full in all early editions of the *Church of Scotland Year Book*.

A system of this kind had obvious disadvantages. Stipend was always a year late. You couldn't even begin to calculate the amount due for 'crop and year 1965' until after March 1966. On the other hand the system did mean that the Minister shared the fortunes of those among whom he worked. In days of depression the stipend fell; in days of prosperity it rose. Victual is a meaningful standard – a boll of oats will provide the same number of bowls of porridge no matter how the pound stands in relation to the dollar.

Statutory Endowments

The Industrial Revolution in Scotland was responsible for a great movement of population and many of the new communities were far from the exiting parish churches. So new parishes *quoad sacra* had to be erected. There was no teind from which to provide stipend for these. In such cases it was made a condition of the erection of a new charge that there be provided sufficient endowment to produce an income of at least £120 per annum for stipend, and this came to be known as the statutory endowment.

It was further required that this be in the form of feu-duties and ground-annuals – the supreme gilt-edged security of that day. Here too we have suffered today from the compulsory redemption of these at a fraction of what they originally cost.

The ancient patrimony of the Kirk has dwindled through forces outwith her control and new sources of income are having to be found if we are to maintain our proud boast of providing Gospel ordinances for the people in every parish in Scotland through a territorial ministry.

32

WHAT WAS THE
VOLUNTARY PRINCIPLE?

IN the previous answer we saw how the business of providing for the ministry was organised in those congregations which had access to the ancient patrimony of the Scottish Kirk, the teind. We turn now to those bodies which in course of the eighteenth century left the fellowship of the National Church and which consequently had no endowments of any kind.

Let us summarise the position in regard to these denominations. In 1733 the first great secession occurred. The Church that came into being that year was unhappily split some 14 years later, continuing in two main branches until 1820 when, after a highly complicated series of splittings and unitings, it was knit together again as the United Secession Church. In 1761 the Relief Church was founded, similar on the temporal side of its life to the Secession body. In 1847 Secession and Relief united to form the United Presbyterian Church, the former bringing 400 and the latter 118 congregations into the union. In 1843 occurred the Disruption leading to the formation of the Free Church. In 1900 Free and UP united to become the United Free Church of Scotland. And, of course, in 1929 all came together as the re-united Church of Scotland.

UP – The Voluntary Principle

In the early days of their history these 500 congregations which came together to form the UP Church must have faced a very acute problem so far as finance was concerned. At a time when congregational giving was practically unknown, they had to raise from within their membership the capital funds necessary to build churches and manses, as well as ongoing income to maintain the property and to pay stipends. That they were able to do this so quickly and so adequately produced a no small feeling of pride, alongside which went a sense of bitterness against anything remotely concerned with the State. Naturally enough too, the bitterness extended to include the methods used by those remaining within the shelter of the establishment. The very idea of endowment was anathema.

Hence the attitude of quite belligerent 'voluntaryism' which characterised many of these congregations – and can be detected in their successors sometimes even today. Treating of this subject in an official publication, it is said:

> *Christian Churches are required to regard provision for the support of their ministers as part of their Christian duty, and are prohibited from transferring this duty to the State. When this is called voluntary giving it is not meant that the contribution is optional so that the Christian disciple is at liberty to give or not to give as he chooses, but that the obligation does not arise from civil statute, but solely from the law of Christ.*

You could not ask for anything stronger or straighter than that.

It was in keeping with this declaration that in 1929 one or two congregations of this tradition agreed to enter into the Union only on receiving written assurance that never in any time coming would they be required to accept any form of endowment over which the State might seem to have some control. So that there could be no danger of 'tainted' money of this kind coming in the form of 'Aid' to such a congregation, it has always been the practice that any free balance of standardised stipend is not put into the general Stipend Fund but is allocated to specific congregations within the area of preference.

The Augmentation Fund

As well as adhering to the voluntary principle, those early congregations of the Secession accepted that the strong were under obligation to help the weak, and they exemplified this in the field of stipend through what came to be called the 'Augmentation Fund'. This Fund was officially set up in 1868 under a special committee whose business it was to ingather contributions from those congregations that could afford to give them, and to administer these through a system of supplements to the lower-paid Ministers so that none received less than £160 per annum.

UP congregations always paid their Ministers direct, and a peculiarity of their system, which many a Minister has blessed on coming to a new charge (if not on departing), was that stipend was usually paid a quarter in advance.

Free – The Sustentation Fund

At the Disruption some 450 Ministers left the Establishment and the question of how they were to be maintained presented the new Church with a problem of breathtaking proportions. Not only had an answer to be found – it had to be found immediately. The fact that so many of the people were behind their Ministers in their determination to found a new church was really an aggravation of the problem, for it meant that the congregation too would be homeless. Not only had manse families to be fed, property had to be acquired as well. As explained in the Answer on the Deacons' Court (page 83), thanks to the genius of Thomas Chalmers an answer was found.

That answer consisted in the creation of the Sustentation Fund to which every congregation contributed according to its means. Out of this fund there was paid to each Minister an annual sum which constituted his basic stipend but which might be supplemented by direct giving from his own people. Thus it was ensured that while some Ministers might be reasonably well-off; none would be in want. This basic payment, known as 'the equal dividend', began at £120, rose in 1879 to £160, and there remained steady throughout the remainder of its history.

UF – The Central Fund

For some time after 1900 the two Funds (Augmentation and Sustentation) continued to function side by side without any effort at co-ordination. In those first years after 1900 the whole financial concern of the new body must have been concentrated on the Free Church Case (*qv*) with all its implications. Later, however, the Central Fund was inaugurated and regulations made for it of such a nature as to make it more nearly than ever before a true Minimum Stipend Fund. Certain surpluses were put together and out of the resulting pool Ministers whose total income from all sources was less than £200 received additional payments so graduated that those who had least got most. There was further revision in 1920 and a true minimum stipend was introduced which provided an admirable model for the re-united Church in 1929; and in the next Answer we shall try to bring that story up-to-date.

33
WHAT IS THE MINIMUM STIPEND?

EVERY minister of a charge in the Church of Scotland must, by way of emoluments from all sources, be in receipt of a sum not less than that fixed as the Minimum Stipend for the current year. Payment, which is *de die in diem*, is made monthly into the recipient's bank account, and, wherever it comes from originally, is paid through the Offices. Many Ministers are in receipt of stipends in excess of the Minimum since a congregation able to pay in excess is at liberty to do so provided it makes an appropriate contribution towards Aid. In certain areas and cases supplementary payments are made from the Fund. The Minister of a parish is also entitled to rent and rates free occupancy of a manse, or, where a manse is not available, to the payment of a Manse Allowance. He is also entitled to receive a refund of the expenses incurred in the discharge of his duty 'Listed Expenses'.

When the Churches united in 1929 it was agreed that the principle of a Minimum Stipend should be adopted, and the figure of £300 and a manse was accepted as the best that could be done at the time, though the confident hope was expressed that this could soon be raised to £400 and a manse. In fact twenty years were to elapse before that figure was actually achieved, and in that time a fair amount of inflation had occurred.

Fixing the Minimum

In those early years the business of determining the Minimum was mathematically simple. When the books had been closed at the end of the financial year two calculations were made – the first to discover how much had been contributed during the year by way of Aid (how much was in the kitty), and the second to find out how many Ministers had received in course of the year less than the Minimum and how much less (the total amount of claims on the kitty). If the former exceeded the latter by an appreciable amount, then it was possible to declare an increase in the Minimum Stipend. In those days the increase would be one of £5, or perhaps in a bumper year, as much as £10. All very simple.

Simple, yes – but time-consuming. By the time it was possible to collect the data and make the calculations it was mid-February before the Minimum could be declared and the balances paid to those dependent upon them to bring them up-to-date with their income for the previous year.

In 1956 a welcome change was made when it was agreed that the current year's Minimum would be declared at the October meeting of the Committee and that it would thus be possible for all on the Minimum to receive the full amount due to them in course of the year to which it applied. Then in 1963, with a view to assisting local Treasurers with their budgeting, the time of declaration was brought still further forward to the autumn. A peculiarity has arisen in that the Minimum Stipend is 'declared' by the Committee and the Assembly is informed, but their opinion is not asked. In the early days this was inevitable, but it is no longer so. Somebody will raise the point one of those days!

From All Sources

It will be noted that what is to be taken into account is 'income from all sources'. This has given rise to two questions of great importance.

The first has to do with other sources of income. Let it be that a Minister is a part-time hospital chaplain. Are payments received in respect of this to be included in deciding his income? There were those who said it should. But if you were going to include such payments what of the position of the man who contributed a weekly piece for his local newspaper, or who acted as an external examiner, or who invigilated at the Highers? You were at the head of a slippery slope. It seemed both fair and simple to include only income which followed necessarily from the Minister's induction to his parish.

The second question has to do with special

endowment – for example where a trust fund made provision for an annual payment to the Minister of the Parish of X. Should he not receive such a payment in addition to the Minimum? That had surely been the intention of the donor. If his congregation paid the Minister above the Minimum, he would receive the trust money as a bonus. It seemed unfair that if his congregation was Aid-receiving the trust money should go in effect to the Minimum Stipend Fund. This whole aspect was very widely canvassed in the 1940s in relation to the Pringle Bequest. The facts briefly were that James Pringle had established a very substantial trust fund, one of whose provisions was that all Ministers in the Moray Firth area were to be paid an annual supplement of £x. The trustees held this must mean 'in addition to what he would have received had there been no Pringle Bequest'. The Maintenance of the Ministry held, on the other hand, that this supplement was part of the endowment of the charge and fell to be included in 'all sources'. The issue went to the courts which upheld the position of the Committee. A hard decision that certainly created anomalies, but even more complexities would have followed had the judgment been otherwise.

Special Areas and Cases

The declaration of the Minimum Stipend goes on to add 'with the appropriate additions in the special areas and cases'. This is a reference to a system, from 1977, of Supplementary Payments to Ministers on the Minimum. The special areas are Shetland and Orkney and other islands, with a further addition when it is the only church on the island. The special cases are three in number – the Minister of a charge who during his incumbency has taken on a union or linking, the minister of a Church Extension charge, and the

Minister of a charge deemed by the Committee to be of special or strategic importance.

... and a Manse

In every case a Manse is expected to be provided, free of rent and, it used to be, free of rates, though the present Council tax cancels out this benefit. Where no Manse is available a Manse Allowance (presently fixed at £1300) falls to be paid in lieu. Increasingly Ministers, particularly in urban areas, are indicating a preference for acquiring a house of their own. In such a case where a manse is available, congregations were in 1992 prohibited from paying the Manse Allowance, though, of course, the minister was not bound to inhabit.

... and Expenses

It is hard to believe that it was not until 1957 that approval was given to the idea of refunding to a Minister the expenses incurred in the discharge of his duties – telephone, notepaper and postages, Communion expenses, and a month, now six weeks, holiday supply. It took another four years, and a great deal of arguing, before travelling expenses were added – even for pedal cycles.

What of the Future?

From time to time motions are advanced at the Assembly which would really mark an end of the Minimum Stipend. Quite recently there has been adopted a complicated system of Service Supplements. It is a brave (or a foolish) person who would foretell what the future holds in store. One thing, though, is clear beyond a peradventure – that it will indeed be a good scheme that will serve both the ministry and the Kirk better than the Minimum Stipend has done.

MACHINERY
OF
ADMINISTRATION

A GREAT part of the time of every General Assembly is taken up with matters of the Church's administration – which means, in effect, with receiving and considering reports from Assembly Committees. These bodies, being creatures of the Assembly, have each May to give an account of their stewardship during the previous calendar year and of their programme for the current year and for the days ahead. In particular they have to indicate any new work they mean to undertake and to give a reasonably accurate forecast of the cost likely to be involved.

The Report is printed at length in the Blue Book where it is preceded by a list of Proposed Deliverances. The latter represent a series of motions which the Assembly is being invited to adopt. Each deals with some aspect of the Committee's work and begins 'The General Assembly: …' going on to approve, to note, to note with satisfaction, to authorise, to regret, to deplore, or whatever it may be. At this point the resolution appears in the briefest possible form consistent with clarity, accuracy and adequacy, the argument being developed in full in the Report.

The Committee Convener submits the Report in a short speech, there is an opportunity for questions (which are meant to be for elucidation not for argument), there is a time for a discussion, and then the numbered sections of the Deliverance are taken one at a time, and at that point it is, of course, open to anyone to move a counter-motion or an amendment or to propose an addendum or a deletion.

In what follows there is set forth a brief story of how the Committee structure has emerged and grown over the years by indication of the field of interest of one or two of the Church's main committees with, in most cases, a brief history of how they have come to be what they are today.

34
WHAT ARE THE COMMITTEES OF THE CHURCH?

PROBABLY the most significant change that has overtaken Presbyterianism in the four centuries of its history has been the development, largely in the past half-century, of the Committee system at Assembly level. Alongside the principle of government by a hierarchy of courts – not supplanting these but working in conjunction with them – has grown up a complete range of Committees answerable directly to the General Assembly. Some would say that in the government of the Kirk Presbytery has been replaced by Bureaucracy. This is not so – at least not yet.

How did it happen?

The original concept of Presbyterianism provided for the initiative coming from the perimeter (the parishes), while the centre was primarily a court of appeal whose business it was to ensure that no one got too far out of line. Only within recent years has the practice developed to any extent of the Assembly sending down directives to the Kirk Sessions through the Presbyteries. In the early days the traffic went the other way – a Kirk Session went ahead and did what it thought proper, waiting for Presbytery to pull it up if it had erred. Today the Kirk Session ventures nothing new until Assembly or Presbytery has sent it instructions. A kind of civil service model – as safe and solid as it is lacking in imagination, initiation and drive.

When the Church began to turn its mind to questions larger than those of the running of its parochial affairs – when, for example, it was stirred towards world mission – it had of necessity to find some machinery of administration beyond that of its four courts. These courts, after all, were to govern, not to administer. The executive side of the work was undertaken by the Ministers and Elders in their parishes. The obvious answer to the problem lay in the Assembly itself undertaking the direction of this work and appointing Committees to carry it forward between Assemblies. As these wider interests of the Church developed, the need grew for more Committees until at the present time there are eight Departments with about fifty Committees, each one entrusted with a particular part of the Church's witness and mission. From time to time a review of administration is undertaken, but always with a view to reducing the number of Committees, however unsuccessful they might prove.

How does it work?

The average Board (which may embrace a number of Committees) consists of as many as a hundred members, ministers, elders, deacons and women members. There is a permanent Secretary (usually a Minister) and an office staff. This may seem inordinately large for a committee, but it has always been recognised that if it is to be representative of the Church as a whole, it must contain a fairly wide cross-section of the membership.

When, however, a committee is so large, it is inevitable that the detailed deliberation is done in small sub-committees, and this is how the major committees now function. We have always been fortunate in having so many laymen, specialists in various fields, ready to put their gifts and experience at our disposal, and such men and women can be of inestimable worth in the work of the sub-committees.

Since they are answerable only to the Assembly which meets but once a year, the Committees have to carry through much of their activity on their own authority. But when the Assembly comes around they have to give an account of their stewardship and to gain approval for any major policy-changes contemplated as well as for any substantial new financial commitment undertaken. When you have an Assembly keenly alert and jealous of its powers, the autonomy that may seem to be being usurped by Committees can be more apparent than real.

Does it work efficiently?

On the whole the Committee system works remarkably smoothly. The question of what it costs is quite another matter which we do not propose to tackle here. It is not to be expected that a committee system could be superimposed on a system of courts without occasional friction if not indeed constant irritation and conflict. But they should not clash because strictly they move, largely, in different planes. The business of Church government is still the business of the courts, the business of the committees is administrative and executive. These two aspects, of course, are not always clear-cut or easy to differentiate.

A similar situation exists in national affairs in the distinction between the Government and the Ministries where the latter often seems to be assuming the authority of the former. In this sphere it is interesting to note how quickly the threat of 'a question on the floor of the House' can bring even the most arrogant ministry to see reason. Similarly, the Committees of the Church have always shown a distinct disinclination to join issue with a Presbytery at the bar of the Assembly. Correctly organised, the Committees of the Church offer no threat to the Presbyteries as courts of the Church – not at least if the latter stick up for themselves.

The real danger of the dual interest, it has often seemed to the writer, lies not in the duplication of work by court and committee, but in the possibility of each side shrugging off responsibility on some less than happy issue on the plea that it is for the other party to act. A shared responsibility can so easily be avoided. There should always be a point where, clearly and unequivocally, the buck stops. One thinks of the case of a student who it has become increasingly clear is not cut out for the work of the ministry and who in everyone's interest (including his or her own) should be stopped. He passed through a Selection School, he was nominated by a Presbytery, he is under the care of the College authorities. All are aware of the problem, all share a measure of responsibility, but who is to grasp the nettle? It is so easy for each to step politely aside in the conviction that this is properly the other chap's job. Meanwhile the Kirk is saddled with yet another misfit.

Committees were created to undertake tasks the courts could not properly perform. So long as the courts continue to discharge responsibly their proper function, Bureaucracy can only supplement and need never supplant Presbytery.

35
WHAT IS
PARISH REAPPRAISAL?

ONE of the high hopes inspiring the movement

that united the Churches in 1929 was that it would be possible to reorganise the whole business of the location and distribution of congregations, and thus by the elimination of needless overlapping there would be set free both funds and personnel to be more advantageously deployed in other needier places.

Accordingly the Basis of Union made provision for the creation of an important new committee to be known as the Committee on Union of Congregations and Readjustment of Agencies. The name was soon abbreviated to that of Committee on Readjustment and in everyday usage to simply 'U and R'. For reasons to be discussed later, the name was changed in 1990 so that it is now the 'Reappraisal Committee'. Whatever the name, the business of the committee remains substantially the same, to reorganise congregational structures by uniting, linking, transporting, re-staffing, so as to secure the most economical use of the Kirk's limited resources in personnel and money.

Unions of Congregations

Three main streams converged to form the river of the re-united Church, and although two of these had already been united for close on thirty years there were still in many areas three separate congregations serving one single community – what had formerly been Parish, Free, and UP. When people still felt keenly about the issues that had divided their fathers, it was only natural, if unfortunate, to have a congregation of each persuasion in every area; but these old animosities having become part of history, it seemed reasonable to believe it would be possible to unite some of the smaller units and so release Ministers who could serve the new communities that already by the beginning of the 1930s were mushrooming around our towns and cities.

Within the larger centres of population, the need for readjustment was apparent and undeniable. About the time of the Union, Glasgow boasted a population of a 1,250,000. This is now reduced to roughly 800,000, or two people where there had been three. Besides 400,000 of these are now living in what had been green fields outside the city. This leaves 400,000 in the former city area – or one in place of three. And the three had been overchurched! Large numbers of small struggling congregations existed on one another's doorstep and were, naturally, finding it difficult to survive. In the villages the picture of the two (or even three) distinct congregations catering for a total membership that would scarcely justify one congregation showed little evidence of efficient organisation.

Efforts have been made by Presbyteries in consultation with the Assembly's Committee to effect wherever possible unions of neighbouring congregations. This has rarely proved easy, for along with the ecclesiastical differences there are always in the background personal misunderstandings and petty animosities. Amazing too is the confidence of a vacant congregation that is really down and out that if only they could get a new Minister the whole scene would be transformed. It is encouraging, therefore, to note that since 1929 something like 900 local unions of congregations have taken place.

Linking of Congregations

As time went on it became increasingly apparent that unions alone were not going to be sufficient to solve the man-power problem. In many parts of the country what had become a tiny congregation stood all by itself in a little village. There was no other congregation with which it could unite yet it was hard to justify its continuance as a full charge involving the employment of a full-time Minister. To meet this situation there was evolved the idea of linking – a system whereby two separate communities share a Minister while retaining their own individuality in every other respect – each has its own buildings, kirk session, parish, organisations, finances. Arrangements are made for the hours of worship to allow of a main service in each place every Sunday and about the sharing of responsibility for stipend and manse.

The next step along this road led to the multiple linking where as many as four separate causes are linked under one Minister. There must be a limit to this. Indeed the Committee itself reported to the Assembly of 1969 that the point had been reached in rural areas where 'further progress might be detrimental to the work of the Church'. Yet seven years later their report showed there were 176 fewer Ministers now at work in the rural areas. Fifty years ago there were 61 Ministers working in the Presbyteries of Dumfries and Kirkcudbright (now one), today there are thirty, it being envisaged that the final figure will be 24 of whom 11 will be stationed in one or other of the towns leaving 13 to cope with that great area of rural Scotland

New Kind of Problem

Readjustment and Church Extension are now coming very close together in the centre of our cities where older parts are being redesigned as Comprehensive Development Areas. This can involve decanting families while the work proceeds, but envisages the ultimate return of those who so desire.

Further, the problem as it confronts us today involves the whole strategy of staffing. So, very rightly, there has been brought within the remit of the Committee the oversight and placing of the Diaconate.

A Church which is to survive in a constantly

changing society must ever be looking to its own organisation. Our Kirk's ability to cope with the population problems of the next fifty years will in no small measure depend on how faithfully we tackle the work of reappraisal today.

36
WHO ARE
THE GENERAL TRUSTEES?

THE General Trustees are a body corporate with a perpetual succession and a common seal. They can sue and be sued. They can purchase, acquire, hold and sell, feu and otherwise dispose of lands, and they have all the privileges of a body corporate. No figure has been set determining their size, and in the first place they numbered eleven, but in recent years the body has always consisted of between thirty and forty members, all of them being necessarily Ministers or Elders of the Kirk and all of them being appointed by the Assembly, but (unlike Committee appointments) without limit of time. The Assembly of 1992 imposed in effect an age limit of 75. Also, for the first time it appointed women members – two of them.

The Trustees were created in terms of an Act of Parliament – The Church of Scotland (General Trustees) Order Confirmation Act of 1921. The object was that they might be a holding body for the various investments, particularly the heritable ones, of the Committees of the then Church of Scotland. These various Committees, referred to in the Act as the General Committees of the Church (15 in number), had in the course of the years acquired funds 'which have been invested in heritable properties and investments the titles of which have been taken in names of different sets of trustees' and it had seemed good to the Assembly that the position should be tidied up by the creation of a central body of trustees in whose name would be vested all this property. It would still be held for behoof of each particular Committee, which would continue to have complete direction and control of it.

As constituted under the 1921 Act then, the General Trustees were purely a holding body acting at the behest of the Assembly and its Committees.

Effect of the 1925 Act

In course of the negotiations preceding the Union of 1929 it became clear that the United Free Church would not consider entering into union unless and until the various properties belonging to the Church of Scotland were put fully and directly under her control – that is to say, in effect, until the heritors were finally removed from the scene. Accordingly representations were made at Parliamentary level for an Act to be passed which would have this effect. The property held for behoof of the Church which was to be transferred into the hands of the Trustees was at this time of two kinds – first there were the actual buildings, churches and manses, and also the glebes; and second there was the teind from which stipends derived. The 1925 Act dealt with both of these – it was a Property and Endowments Act.

The heritable property was to be put into a proper state of repair, failing which a sum of money in respect of the extent to which it was deficient was to be paid over. The Church was then able to obtain a Sheriff's Certificate which represented a good and clear title to the property. The teind on the other hand, as explained in the Answer on Victual Stipend (page 117), was converted into a Standard Charge and the right to this was to vest in the Church itself and not in the incumbent for the time being as the custom had been. Thus stipend was 'standardised'. Clearly a change-over of this magnitude required that there be trustees to whom the transference could be made and who would hold in name of the Church. The new body, created only four years before, provided a ready and an adequate answer to the problem. So everything to which the Kirk had a claim, heritable property and standard charge alike, came to be vested in the General Trustees. Opportunity was taken also to transfer to the General Trustees the holding of *quoad sacra* properties which had been held under a variety of local arrangements. There were also some peculiar cases like Burgh Churches and Parliamentary Parishes which were brought under the umbrella. At the time of the Union in 1929, therefore, it could fairly be said that every kind of property in which the Kirk had an interest was wholly under her own direction and control.

The 1925 Act then clearly had the effect of changing out of recognition both the range and the character of the holding activities of the General Trustees. It had the effect also of greatly extending their responsibilities and conferring upon them administrative activities as well as their holding duties – these being subject always to the direction of the Assembly.

The Church of Scotland Trust

In 1932 a further statute was passed – the Church of Scotland Trust Order Confirmation Act. In terms of this legislation a completely new body was created, the Church of Scotland Trust, and to this was to be transferred from the General Trustees all the properties which they were hold-ing in terms of the 1921 Act – that is to say, those in which they were merely a holding and not at all an administrative body. The rather curious situation that emerged was that the General Trustees were created in 1921 to do a specific job; four years later they were given a great many additional duties; and then seven years later still they were relieved of all the original duties.

Amending Acts of one sort and another were passed in 1933, 1957 (two Acts) and 1978, the last-named enabling the Assembly to delegate their powers relative to the disposal of property and the application of proceeds. In respect of monies held for stipend the power was delegated to the Maintenance of the Ministry Committee, in respect of the heritable properties to the General Trustees.

Administrative Functions

In recent years the administrative work of the General Trustees has increased out of recognition. All Church Extension properties, once congregations achieve full status, become the responsibility of the Trustees. Up till then the Home Board had been the responsible authority. Following upon an examination in 1976 it was agreed that a plethora of central bodies were involved in the administration of properties and related funds and this being unsatisfactory the Law, Property Cases and Discipline Committee and the Home Board Property Committee were abolished, the Trustees taking on their functions. Also under their control were brought manses which, though not vested in them, were in terms of their titles under Assembly control. The Trustees also have to approve applications for grants from the Historic Buildings Committee. A building fund previously administered by the Home Board was made over to the Trustees and along with some other funds formed the foundation of the Central Fabric Fund which makes grants to assist in repairs to and maintenance of church property. The Trustees too are now the responsible body to which report has to be made regarding the regular inspection of, and insurance of, churches, halls and manses.

In 1989 a new fund was created called the Consolidated Loan Fund. This was, in effect, a massing of all the funds, capital and interest alike, held for congregations following upon the sale of property. Both the capital and the interest accruing from this massive investment (after allocations to the investing congregations) is used largely to make loans at modest rates of interest to congregations faced with large expenditure on fabric projects.

While not all the property of the Church of Scotland is today vested in the General Trustees, an increasing amount of it is.

37
WHAT IS
WORLD MISSION AND UNITY?

CONSIDERING the enormous enthusiasm which the movement was later to engender, it is hard to believe that the Kirk took its first steps into the field of Foreign Mission enterprise with great hesitation and misgiving – indeed in face of strong opposition. For long after the Reformation the Kirk had been too deeply concerned establishing her own position to give much thought to the far-flung implications of the faith. The same forces that had led to revolution in France combined to arouse the Kirk to a new spiritual awareness. Missionary societies were formed in Glasgow and in Edinburgh and in 1796 overtures in favour of missions came to the Assembly from the Synods of Fife and Moray, the latter containing a proposal that collections should be made for it throughout the Kirk.

The Assembly was not impressed. One did not need to go abroad to find heathen in need of conversion, there were plenty at our doors; the amenities of civilisation should precede the introduction of the Gospel: Church collections were bound by statute to go for support of the poor. The debate concluded in very grand manner, expressing fine sentiments but making no commitment:

While they offer their fervent prayers to Almighty God for the fulfilment of His promise in giving His Son the heathen for an inheritance, they resolve that they will embrace, with zeal and with thankfulness any favourable opportunity for contributing, by their exertions, to the propagation of the Gospel of Christ, which Divine Providence may hereafter open.

And they remitted the matter to a committee.

In spite of so dismal a start, missionary zeal developed and spread till it became the consuming interest in many a congregation, and of all extra-mural activities this was the one towards which the people contributed most generously.

Foreign Mission

By the time of the 1929 Union, both branches of the Church were heavily committed in the Foreign Mission field, each conducting extensive work mainly in Africa and India. It was bound to happen that as the work grew and congregations began to be formed the organisation was built on Presbyterian foundations so that by 1962 there were no fewer than 16 Presbyteries (with such unlikely names as Bengal, Rajputana, the Gold Coast) and involving just over 100 missionaries sent out from, and, in the last resort, answerable to, Edinburgh. Twelve years later the Presbyteries had vanished and the number of missionaries had been drastically curtailed. This was attributable to the fact that as the work developed the local church became stronger, so that we no longer sent out missionaries to convert the heathen but rather to co-operate with the local church in its evangelical outreach.

As well as missionary activity among the heathen, the Kirk had long been engaged overseas in two different directions. There was work among the Jews – an outreach extending to Israel as well as centres throughout Europe. There was – and still is – a Presbytery of Jerusalem. This work was entrusted to the Jewish Mission Committee. Then there was the work among expatriated Scots in the colonies and throughout Europe. The work was in the hands of 'Colonial and Continental'.

In 1964 a large-scale reorganisation of office administration was undertaken, one of the consequences being the setting-up of the Overseas Council to embrace Foreign Mission, Jewish Mission, Colonial and Continental as well as two smaller committees, the Scots Memorial Jerusalem, and Inter-Church Aid and Refugee Service.

World Mission and Inter-Church Relations

The decision referred to immediately above had the additional effect of bringing together the new Overseas Council and the Committee on Inter-Church Relations. This seemed reasonable since much of the work was no longer of a missionary character. The Committee which bore the latter name, however, had been seen as belonging to the General Interests department. It was concerned in a general supervisory way with particular conversations that might be in progress at any time with some other denomination, but more directly it was concerned with the position of the Kirk in relation to the various ecumenical councils (BCC, WCC, SCC, *etc*) that were occupying so much of the stage at that time.

The two sections of the new department never fused. Each did its own job, and apart from presenting their report to the Assembly under one umbrella and sharing the same office space, there has been little connection. One matter that caused considerable difficulty had to do with the membership fees payable to these ecumenical bodies. As the activities of these organisations expand, so their bills increase and the member-churches are faced with ever-larger assessments. These had still to be presented to the Assembly by the General Administration Committee, although it had no control whatever over the spending. No Committee has.

Board of World Mission

Today we have a Board of World Mission to enable the Kirk at every level to experience and enjoy being part of the world-wide Church, sharing in the mission of God, as partners with the other Churches in the work of seeking God's Kingdom on Earth.

It operates today through committees bearing the names Executive, Finance, Global, Local Involvement, Personnel, Sub-Saharan Africa and the Caribbean, Middle East and North Africa, Asia, Europe, United Kingdom and Eire, and Women's Business Committee.

In the actual field it has nearly 100 partners (as missionaries are now called) about 70 of them serving under the direction of national churches in 15 or so countries overseas, with twelve ministers on mainland Europe attached to the Presbytery of that name, and about 14 people in Israel linked to the Presbytery of Jerusalem.

THE RIGHT
TO DIFFER

THE Scot has always inclined to be an individualist, and nowhere has this been more clearly exemplified than in his attitude toward the matters of the faith. There are those who would contend that this individualism sprang from religious roots, and it is certainly true that the Scottish Reformation with its horror of the idea of intervention by priests and saints and the Blessed Virgin into the relationship between a man and his Creator was responsible for an atmosphere where the individual saw himself holding a unique position that no other could share. In any case, whatever the reason, there can be no denying that the Scot has always bitterly resisted any kind of regimentation – nobody is going to tell him what he is to believe. It is he and he alone who will have to answer to God at the Great Day of Judgment.

One thing which the Presbytery of today does very badly is to parade on ceremonial occasions. Try as you will to get the members lined up neatly in pairs *juniores priores* before they set off on their march, they will, within a few yards, be straggling along in a broken disorderly column. It goes against the Scots inclination to march in line on any occasion, least of all on an ecclesiastical occasion!

The cause of the Covenanters was continuously bedevilled by their inability to reach agreement, to come to a common mind. Even when it came to a battle they insisted on fighting it on the principle that each man did his own thing – with the most disastrous results. That spirit continued down into the eighteenth century and goes some way to explain many divisions of the period. Indeed the history of the Scottish Church throughout a long spell is simply a story of splinter groups.

In the following pages we take a look at some of these divisions, for they make an intensely interesting study. There was Ebenezer Erskine and the First Secession and the multitude of groups into which that divided itself. Then a word is said about Thomas Gillespie and the Relief Church which, strangely enough, held together as a single unit until 1847 when it united with the by then largely reunited First Seceders.

Our attention then turns to the Disruption, to the events which led up to it, and to some of the significant things that followed upon it. In a concluding Answer (page 172), we look at what occurred in 1929 when the various strands were knit together again in the one Church of Scotland as we know it today.

38

WHO WAS
EBENEZER ERSKINE?

IT is amazing how often an event of major historical significance has found itself triggered off by some comparatively trivial incident. The occurrence in 1733 of the first secession from the Church of Scotland was to make a profound impression on Scottish Church life for many a generation, but it all arose out of an event of so little seeming importance as scarce to merit recording.

As has been explained elsewhere, patronage was restored in 1712, but there was a widespread feeling against it, so much so that many heritors who had the right to present delayed doing so within the stipulated six months so that under the *ius devolutum* the duty of filling the vacancy fell to the Presbytery. By 1730 this was becoming a common practice, but different Presbyteries adopted different ways of discharging their duty and it was felt that a standard practice should be followed. Accordingly an overture was presented to the Assembly of 1731, passed by it as an Interim Act, and sent down to Presbyteries under the Barrier Act.

The proposal was that in such a case appointment to the vacant charge should be made upon a Call from the Heritors of the Parish (being Protestants) along with the Elders. The nomination was then to be put to the congregation, and if any member thought to disapprove he was at liberty to do so, giving in his reasons to the Presbytery, and that court would be judge of the validity of these. It seemed a reasonable scheme, at least as a beginning, for it put it within the power of the congregation for good and sufficient reason to stop an appointment while at the same time preventing causeless prejudices prevailing.

Enter Ebenezer Erskine

Of all who opposed the new Act none was more vociferous than the recently inducted Minister of Stirling, Ebenezer Erskine. Born in Dryburgh in 1680 of parents who had been persecuted as Covenanters, he had until the previous year been Minister at nearby Portmoak. The cause of his disquiet was the continuing place of importance accorded to the Heritors.

As indicated, however, the Act was duly passed, continuing the Heritors alongside the Elders. On the following Sunday from his pulpit in Stirling Erskine made a further blistering attack on what by then had become the law of the Kirk.

As it happened he was Moderator of the Synod at this time and as such had the duty of preaching at its opening session in the autumn in St John's Kirk in Perth. Here he saw fit to renew his attack in even more bitter terms. He declared that 'whatever Church authority may be in that Act yet it lacks the authority of the Son of God', going on to make the remarkable claim:

> Seeing the Reverend Synod had put me in this place where I am in Christ's stead I must be allowed to say of this Act what I apprehend that Christ Himself would say of it, 'Inasmuch as ye have done it to one of these little ones ye did it to me'.

The Road to Separation

It is just possible that had Erskine been allowed a brief cooling-off period he himself might have come to see just how intolerant and arrogant was the position he had assumed. He was not to be allowed this, though, for immediately the Synod met for the despatch of business a member objected that in his sermon the Moderator had said things that were offensive, and a committee was appointed to consider the matter. Their report was to the effect that the preacher had been disrespectful to the Assembly, and after protracted discussion it was agreed that for this he should be censured. Against which judgment Erskine took appeal to the Assembly.

At the Assembly of 1733 Erskine appeared, supported by three friends. He claimed that he was bound to say what he did, and that in any case there was nothing in the Act which said that you couldn't preach against it. The Assembly found that parts of the sermon were offensive and liable to disturb the peace of the Church and that he should be rebuked. But before this could be done Erskine, supported by his friends, laid a document on the table and departed. Though the document was highly discourteous, the authors flatly refused to withdraw it.

All very exciting, but the idea was growing that a molehill was being allowed to develop into a mountain and efforts at reconciliation were made. At the August Commission, Erskine read a paper which hurled defiance at authority. This resulted in the four Ministers being suspended from the exercise of their ministerial functions. They completely ignored the suspension, continuing with business as usual. At its next meeting the Commission had no alternative but to sever the pastoral tie in each case.

On 5th December of that same year (1733) the four, who had now been joined by Ebenezer's younger brother, Ralph (of Dunfermline), met at Gairney Bridge near Kinross and after prayer and solemn discussion constituted themselves the Associate Presbytery, later to become the Associate Synod, and later still the Church of the First Secession.

Efforts at reconciliation went on unabated, even to the point when they became efforts at appeasement. But Erskine was not to be appeased. For a long time, he said, he had been swimming against the current in the Kirk. Then in 1736 the group published their *Judicial Testimony*, which showed just how desperately deep and wide was the chasm which now separated them from the Establishment.

At the same time some very awkward situations were arising. Dunfermline was a collegiate charge. Ralph Erskine, though now no longer one of the Ministers, fulminated against the Establishment in the morning while his colleague defended it in the afternoon. Ebenezer banned five of his Elders because they would not accept Secession principles. But, of course, they were not his Elders by now!

This kind of thing could not be allowed to continue indefinitely so at long last in May 1740 the General Assembly pronounced sentence of deposition against the seceding group. So a situation was created of the kind, 'Over to you, Mr Erskine'.

39
WHAT WAS AN ANTIBURGHER?

TO anyone unversed in the nice distinctions in which Scottish Church history abounds, the word 'Antiburgher' may not have a very obvious religious ring to it, yet for many years the mere mention of the name could be enough to start an argument – of the most heated kind at that – among a group of devoted Churchmen.

In 1733 had occurred the first secession from the Church of Scotland, the new Church assuming the title of Associate Synod. This body was no more than established when it found itself involved in a controversy over the Burgess Oath of 1746, with a consequent split into two bitterly hostile camps, Burghers and Antiburghers. For fifty years this state of affairs continued until in 1797 this group divided into Auld Lichts and New Lights, to be followed a few years later by a similar division in the ranks of their opposite numbers. Thus what had at the first constituted a comparatively small group hiving off from the main body became four distinct denominations. And all within a single lifetime.

Causes of Secession

In the early eighteenth century the Church of Scotland embraced within its fold the whole population of the land with the exception of small companies of Episcopalians and of Roman Catholics on the one side and a coterie of Cameronians on the other. It was inevitable that within so comprehensive a body there should be represented vastly different shades of opinion on a wide variety of topics. In particular there were divergent views on the relation of Church and State, on theological questions, and on the freedom of the individual within the fellowship and discipline of the Church. So long as people do not feel too strongly on issues of that kind, the unity of the whole can be maintained. Diversity lends colour and interest to unity. But when conscience creeps in a new scene emerges.

It was a question regarding the relation of Church and State that raised the 1733 issue which was to lead to the deposition of certain Ministers and the creation of the Associate Synod. It was the Act anent Calls, attached as that was to the patronage problem that inspired Ebenezer Erskine to the strong stand he was to take. Matters were further complicated by a question regarding the enrolment of Mr Stark who, in face of strong local feeling, had been inducted to Kinross, but whom the Presbytery refused, in spite of an Assembly injunction, to enrol as one of its members. The aftermath of the Porteous Riots added its quota. A proclamation for the discovery of the leaders in the affair was ordered to be read in every pulpit in Scotland on the first Sunday of each month for a year. Here was a clear enough indication of whither the Church State was heading.

Then there was the question of how far the member – or Minister – of the Church was to be subject to the discipline of its courts in matters of conscience. The Assembly after due process had passed an Act – was it for Erskine, however strongly he might feel, to use the occasion of a crowded Communion service to direct a tirade against it? Erskine's plea was that conscience must come before conformity. Must it?

Behind all of this, of course, lay profound theological differences. An acute situation arose in 1720 with the appearance of a book – *The Marrow of Modern Divinity* – which in that same year was condemned by the Assembly. Immediately a protest was lodged by twelve Ministers, soon to become famous as 'the Marrow Men', and they were censured by the Assembly for their pains. Again to the more zealous it seemed an outrage that the Marrow Men should be subjected to strictures for adhering to the true tenets of the faith while Professor Simson and his modern heresies were protected.

The Burgess Oath

The Associate Synod, having been duly formed, quickly flourished, the number of Secession congregations increasing steadily. The trouble about people who suffer from an inclination to separate themselves because they feel very strongly about some small point is that ere long they can be counted on to find some new issue on which opinion can be divided − conscientious opinion at that. It was unfortunate that such opportunity for dispute and controversy should have been provided only seven years after the Seceders had properly got going − in terms of the Burgess Oath.

Following upon the failure of the Jacobite Rising of 1745 and bearing in mind the close connection between the Stuart dynasty and the Episcopal Church, the authorities designed an Oath which every burgess had to subscribe in which, among other things, he had to undertake that 'he professed and allowed within his heart the true religion presently professed within the realm and authorised by the laws thereof'. What in more specific terms did that mean?

According to Erskine and his ilk there was no problem. The 'true religion' could mean only one thing − the form of worship they themselves professed and practised − and one surely need have no scruples about swearing allegiance to that. In the view of the other group, more ready perhaps to find occasion for offence than to seek a way of avoiding it, this was sheer evasion, hypocrisy, casuistry, the 'true religion' for purposes of the oath could mean only the religion recognised by law, to wit that of the Established Church. How could honest men who for conscience' sake had come out of that Church, profess allegiance to the religion which it represented?

In 1736 the matter came before the Associate Synod when, after heated debate, it was resolved that the Burgess Oath should not be taken by any of their members, and that any who had already signed it were to appear before their Kirk Sessions and make confession of their defection.

The following year when the Synod met again the debate was even more acrimonious ending in open rupture, the two parties separating under the names of Burghers and Antiburghers. The latter, not content with separation, went so far as to summon the members of the other group to their bar, and on their non-appearance to treat them as contumacious, even passing upon them the sentence of the greater excommunication.

To us the whole thing would seem so utterly petty and trivial, if it were not so tragically unnecessary. It is hard for us to believe how seriously the matter was taken by those concerned. It is recorded that Ralph Erskine's son, a Minister of the Antiburgher persuasion, lay sick and dying, but would not allow his father, a detested Burgher, to pray at his bedside.

The breach was to remain open for 100 years and it is sad but true to say that during a great part of that time the attitude of the two branches towards one another was at least as uncharitable as it was to the Establishment from which they had come.

40
WHAT WAS AN AULD LICHT ANTIBURGHER?

ONCE Burghers and Anti-burghers had got over their first enthusiasm for miscalling and excommunicating one another, they continued to offer their separate witness for exactly half a century.

The Lifter Controversy

In 1782 the peace of the Antiburgher camp was disturbed with what came to be known as the Lifter Controversy. David Smyton had gone to be Minister at Kilmaurs in 1740 when the Associate Synod was formed, and over the years had acquired responsibilities also at Fenwick, Dalry, and Kilwinning. Came the Breach, his first sympathies were with the Burghers, but he quickly came to see the error of his ways and after due confession and promise of compliance the Antiburgher Presbytery of Edinburgh received him into that fold.

At this time it would seem that within that body the practice was for the celebrant not to lift the elements at the celebration of communion, and to this in 1782 Seyton took grave exception. It was not just that he preferred to 'lift' – he insisted that *all* were to prefer to 'lift'. Jesus, he said, took bread before He blessed it, and we should follow His example. When the matter came before the Synod they took, for them, a remarkably open view, the leader at that time, Adam Gib, insisting on tolerance. For Smyton this simply would not do – for him the question was 'whether the example of the Great Head of the Church is to be rule of administration or not'.

Though heavily defeated in the Synod, Smyton seems to have found sufficient support in a few parishes in North Ayrshire and in Falkirk to encourage the formation of a Presbytery of Antiburgher Lifters – a body due to have a short if stormy life-history.

New Light dawns on the Burghers

In 1795 Mr John Fraser of Auchtermuchty made representation to the Burgher Synod that there should be a relaxation of their Formula, especially in its allegiance to the Covenants. A Committee appointed to look into the matter agreed that there were differences of opinion, but pleaded for forbearance. And in the meantime explanations and reservations were appended to the two offending paragraphs. It is worthy of noting that a stage had apparently been reached within so rigid a sect that they recognised that 'good and faithful men' could genuinely see things differently and that provision should be made for this.

This degree of tolerance, however, was not universally shared, so that out of 47 petitions before the Synod in 1797 only nine were in favour of change. And two years later a group broke away so as to demonstrate their 'unqualified adherence to our principles'. They called themselves the 'Original Burgher Synod'; others have called them the 'Auld Licht Burghers'.

... and on the Antiburghers

The issue that was to split the Burghers the way we have seen had in fact arisen even earlier among their opposite numbers. As early as 1791 two probationers made it a condition of their going forward to ordination that in putting the second question (that accepting the whole doctrine of the Confession) the Moderator would explain that they had reservations anent this. Clearly this raised a most serious issue which in fact was referred to the Synod. In 1796 this passed a Declaratory Act saying *inter alia* that while not implying 'the smallest reflection upon the venerable compilers of the Confession', the degree of light enjoyed by them seemed to have led them to invest civil rulers with a degree of power inconsistent with 'the spirituality, freedom, and independence of the Kingdom of Christ'.

In 1799, as a result of the protracted labours of a special committee, there was produced a new 'Acknowledgment of Sins and Engagement of Duties'. As was to be expected this produced a howl of protest – one of the loudest howlers being Thomas McCrie, one of the two probationers whose reservations had set the whole train of events in motion. So a revised Testimony was produced in 1804. This made the surprising claim for the Westminster Confession that it is not 'all the rule of what we are bound to believe, but a public declaration of what we do believe', and went on 'to claim the right in view of any further light which may afterwards arise from the Word of God to change its mind on any article of divine truth'. In this way, using the idea of how a new light can give us a completely new picture, they were able at one and the same time to bind themselves to, and to free themselves from, the objectionable articles of the Confession. A recipe had been found for a cake which you can eat and still have in the larder.

When in 1806 the Testimony was finally adopted by the Antiburgher Synod, a group of six Ministers protested and separated. Their leader was Archibald Bruce of Whitburn. In the eyes of these six their departure had not created a new body – they, in fact, constituted the small continuing remnant of the original body – hence, probably their choice of title – Constitutional Associate Synod. For all that they will always be known as the 'Auld Licht Antiburghers'.

It could be said that, in spite of appearances to the contrary, the seceders of 1733 were inspired by an intense religion conservatism, and in this sense the Auld Light Antiburghers could claim to be their true successors – a body which in a day of intellectual fervent was seeking to be more true to the standards of their fathers than the said fathers had ever been. Indeed it would not be difficult to trace their genealogy straight to the Covenanters.

We have seen then how the Secession Church of 1733 (the Associate Synod) had by 1806 become four: the original Burgher Synod (the Auld Licht Burghers); the Associate Synod (the New Light Burghers); the Constitutional Associate Presbytery (the Auld Licht Anti-burghers); and the General Associate Synod (the New Light Antiburghers).

Mercifully in the Providence of God within twenty years there was to begin a story of re-union, though sadly there was almost invariably a remnant. The tale is told of man who explained to his friend that there used to be two Churches in his village, till they had a union, and now there were three. The tale is also told of the man who showed his friend some of the half-dozen churches spread throughout his little village. 'Yours must be a very religious people,' was the not unnatural rejoinder. 'No,' replied the native, 'juist sheer damn thrawn.'

41
WHAT WAS
THE RELIEF CHURCH?

WE have traced in some detail how tension was growing over unpopular appointments to parishes and the consequent troubles over the induction of Ministers in such cases leading up to the crisis at Torphichen when the Presbytery flatly refused to act. We come now to the story which provides the background to the Presbytery of Relief which for 86 years was to represent an independent denomination within the fold of Scottish Presbyterianism. The inception of this body is generally referred to as the Second Secession.

Early in 1751 Mr Andrew Richardson, a Minister at Broughton, was presented with all due legal formality by the patron to the vacant Parish of Inverkeithing. He was an excellent Minister in every way; he had appeared very acceptable to the people until it was learned that he was to be appointed under the patronage system; when finally he had been inducted he proved not only an able but also a popular Minister. Those in the parish determined to fight patronage, however, found themselves opposed to Mr Richardson. They prepared a Call to a Mr William Adam, Minister of a dissenting congregation in England.

Problem for Dunfermline Presbytery

The Presbytery of Dunfermline, when they came to consider the matter, found themselves with on the one hand a legal presentation and on the other a Call which had no legal standing whatever. It might well have seemed that they had no alternative but to proceed on the strength of the former. This, however, they delayed doing, sending instead a committee to Inverkeithing to discover how far Mr Richardson's appointment was likely to meet with favour. That they found it would not be universally acceptable is not surprising – what is surprising is that they found very little evidence of hostility to it. The Presbytery then referred the whole affair to the Commission of Assembly.

The matter was before the Commission in November and again the following March, and finally it came before the Assembly itself in May of that same year, 1752. By this time it was abundantly clear that this was to be a test case which would decide with some finality what was to be the Church's attitude to patronage, but it would also determine the more urgent question of how far the individual was under obligation to carry out the orders of the superior courts of the Church.

The Assembly agreed without a division that Mr Richardson's induction must go forward and went on to order the Presbytery to meet at Inverkeithing the following Thursday for this purpose. The quorum of Presbytery was increased from the customary three to five. Further, each member of Presbytery was to appear at the bar of Assembly the following day to give an account of his obedience in the matter.

The case in favour of this determined attitude had been put by William Robertson of Gladsmuir, later to be Principal of Edinburgh University. His argument was that if Ministers and Presbyteries were to be at liberty to disobey the orders of the Assembly, that would be the end of Presbyterianism. Discipline was of the essence of its system, and when this could no longer be enforced General Assemblies might as well cease to exist. Those on the other side held out for the liberty of the individual conscience against all regimentation, including orders from the Assembly. This was the freedom the Reformation had secured, and it must be preserved at all costs. It was the age-old tension of law against liberty – both essential elements in any healthy society. The stage was set for a real test.

Mr Thomas Gillespie

On the day appointed four Ministers appeared at Inverkeithing and not being the prescribed quorum they were unable to proceed. When, the following day, this was reported, the Assembly, recognising that it had to assert its authority, resolved that it had to depose one of the recalcitrant Ministers. By unanimous decision Mr Thomas Gillespie, Minister at Carnock, was selected to 'carry the can'.

There seems little doubt that Gillespie was generally regarded as having been the ringleader in this affair, though one less likely for such a role would be hard to imagine. He had begun his studies for the Established Kirk, had transferred for some time to training for the Secession Church, and having completed his course under an English Independent was ordained by a group of Ministers south of the Border. A man of no particular brilliance, he was yet a most faithful and devoted Minister, more concerned for the effectiveness of a Gospel ministry than for the tradition or polity of a national Church. It was the fact of his suffering deposition that brought him into prominence as a martyr suffering for conscience' sake.

For a time after his deposition Gillespie preached in the open air and in various temporary meeting-places, but in time a church was built in Dunfermline and his ministry there attracted a considerable congregation. More than once in the years that followed an attempt was made to have him restored, but, largely because he himself would never apply, nothing came of these efforts.

Presbytery of Relief

It was on 22nd October 1761, nine years after his deposition, that Gillespie along with two other Ministers of like persuasion constituted themselves the Presbytery of Relief. His colleagues in this step were a Mr Collier, an English dissenter who had established a meeting-house at Colinsburgh, scene of an unpopular settlement, and Mr Thomas Boston who was conducting services in Jedburgh in similar circumstances. The new denomination quickly grew so that by 1847, when it joined with others to form the UP Church, it could boast 136 congregations.

The name may strike us as odd, but to the

founders its significance was clear – the new denomination existed for 'the relief of Christians oppressed in their Christian privileges'. Its emphasis upon evangelism as against organisation distinguished it from the Establishment; its lack of enthusiasm for the Covenants distinguished it from the First Seceders; and for its day it showed a wondrous liberality in its readiness to admit to its Communion tables members of other denominations. It continued one and undivided to the end.

It is interesting that Gillespie should to the last have retained a profound regard for the Church of Scotland, so that on his death-bed he advised his own congregation to seek re-admission to it – as in fact they did. One cannot but think he would have rejoiced in the Union of 1929.

42
WHAT WAS THE TEN YEARS' CONFLICT?

THE 'Ten Years' Conflict' is the title commonly given to the strife that took place within the Church of Scotland in the years 1834–43 which culminated in the Disruption. A conflict presumes combatants, and there were opposing camps here. For a very long time two contradictory influences had been at work in the Kirk, but it was as the nineteenth century advanced that the lines of separation became much more clearly defined and the position of the two sides more deeply entrenched. They had come to be known as Moderates and Evangelicals, the former representing the conservative element, always inclined to be strong in any ecclesiastical set-up, people who looked upon any excess of zeal as something of an extravagance to be discouraged; while the Evangelicals were the progressive party including most of those working in the growth areas, the Chapels of Ease.

The leader of the Moderates was Andrew Thomson, Minister of the fine new church of St George's in the midst of Edinburgh's New Town and including in its congregation the most highly intellectual and cultured group which Scotland could produce; and at the other extreme the Evangelical leader, Thomas Chalmers, Minister of the new Glasgow charge of St John's, a parish which probably embraced more poverty, squalor and dereliction than any comparable acreage in all of Scotland, or possibly of Europe.

As has been said, the battlelines had been forming up for some years, issue being joined mainly on matters connected with the sorry business of patronage. It was, however, in 1834 that the Evangelical party, having achieved a majority of votes in the Assembly passed two momentous Acts and the battle was on in earnest. But now it had become a battle between the Kirk and the courts of the land.

The Veto Act

It was well established law that when a presentation was made to a parish the Presbytery had the right and duty to take the presentee on trials with a view to satisfying itself that he was qualified for the appointment. Being qualified had till then been construed as referring to academic qualifications. The object of the Veto Act passed in 1834 was to include acceptability to the congregation as a necessary qualification. The Act ordained:

> ... it shall be an instruction to Presbyteries that if, at the moderating of a Call to a vacant charge, the major part of the male heads of families, members of the vacant congregation, and in full communion with the church, shall disapprove of the person in whose favour the Call is proposed, such disapproval shall be sufficient ground for the Presbytery rejecting such person.

In October of that same year, the parish of Auchterarder having fallen vacant, the patron, the Earl of Kinnoull, made presentation to Mr Robert Young. Rebellion was in the air at Auchterarder so that only three people signed the Call, and out of 330 heads of families 287 turned out to record their thumbs-down. Appeals on some trivial procedural matters took the case to the Assembly of 1835 which instructed the Presbytery to proceed in terms of the new Act. This they obediently did, rejecting Mr Young. An action was raised in the Court of Session by the patron. After avizandum and by eight votes to five, the Court found against the Presbytery. The Assembly of 1838, when it met a few weeks later, passed a resolution that 'in all matters touching the government, doctrine and discipline of this Church her judicatories possess an exclusive jurisdiction founded on the Word of God'. They also decided to appeal to the House of Lords – though the two decisions might seem to contradict one another. The Lords found in favour of Mr Young, declared the Veto Act illegal and pronounced the term 'qualifications' to be a technical one referring only to the presentee's life, literature and doctrine.

Even more unhappy were the circumstances surrounding the case of Marnoch in the Presbytery of Strathbogie. Here the majority of the Presbytery accepted and acted upon the decisions that came from the civil courts and thereby put themselves in contempt so far as the instructions of the Assembly were concerned. The possibilities of that situation were terrifying and the day came when the offending Ministers were suspended from office and others appointed to enter their parishes and function in their stead. Against which, of course, they went to the Court of Session (it was becoming a well-trodden path) and had the proposed intruders interdicted. The fact, however that a man had been interdicted from the pulpit didn't prevent him preaching in the public square. A most unhappy affair which ended in the induction of a Minister by half of the Presbytery after the entire congregation had solemnly walked out of the church.

The Chapels Act

That same year 1834 saw another Act go on the statute-book – an innocent enough affair it might have seemed – the Chapels Act. As has been explained elsewhere, the Chapels of Ease that were the product of the great population explosion of the early part of the century suffered many constitutional disadvantages. The new Act altered all that. They were now to have their own Kirk Sessions, parishes were to be delimited for them, their Ministers were to sit in the Church courts. The voice of moderatism was raised in protest – these changes, they said, were very nice and very proper, but it was not for the Church at her own hand to alter law that was not of her own creating. They lost by 152 votes to 103.

A group of Seceders in the parish of Stewarton had in 1839 returned to the Establishment and their Minister had been granted a seat in Presbytery. Part of the parish of Stewarton was being carved out for his parish when they were interdicted by the principal heritor, Cunningshaw of Lainshaw. The case went before a full Court of Session, where it was decided, again by eight to five, that the Church courts had no power of themselves to create parishes *quoad sacra* or to admit the Ministers of such as members of Presbytery.

Founding on this judgment a certain Minister, who was being libelled by his Presbytery for incurring debt, appealed to the Court of Session for interdict on the ground that the court which tried him was vitiated by the presence of Chapel Ministers. He was hailed before the Assembly and summarily deposed from the Ministry – not for debt, but for taking his case to the civil courts.

It is quite impossible to condense a ten year war into one brief Answer. Enough has been written, perhaps, to show how the battlelines were drawn, to indicate some of the areas where the conflict was at its most bitter, and to suggest that some kind of disruption was inescapable.

43
WHAT WAS
THE DISRUPTION?

'CAN two walk together,' asked the prophet Amos, 'except they be agreed?' The answer is that they can do so for a time, none too happily, but that sooner or later they must split and go their separate ways. Certainly that was the case in relation to Moderate and Evangelicals in the Kirk of the early nineteenth century. Over a long period relations had been strained, the divisions in the ranks becoming even more obviously defined, by 1834 they were engaged in open conflict on important issues, by 1843 the parting of the ways was inevitable.

We have in the previous answer seen something of the events that immediately led to that parting. It occurred when it did principally because of three things that happened in the spring of that year. First, judgment was given in the House of Lords in the Second Auchterarder Case. This had to with the proposal that Mr Young be allowed to enjoy the stipend and other benefits of the living so long as he was not Minister of the charge. Their Lordships were unanimous that this would not do, the Presbytery must take the presentee on trials and if satisfied must induct. The second factor had to do with an appeal addressed to the Sovereign through Sir James Graham based upon the Claim of Right.

By the spring it had become evident that no help was to come from that quarter. And the third was the Judgment of the Court of Session in the Stewarton case that the Ministers of the Chapels of Ease had no right to sit in the Church courts. Separation could not be put off any longer.

It has been suggested that at one stage the Evangelical party hoped to secure such an ascendancy in the coming Assembly as to be able to carry a motion which would completely sever the Church's connection with the State. A motion so momentous, however, could not become law in that way – it would be quite ineffectual until it had been down under the Barrier Act, and it was realised it would not suffer such treatment.

As it was, there was great controversy in Presbyteries when the time came to elect commissioners to the Assembly. Some of the Presbyteries, in view of the Stewarton judgment, had disenfranchised the Chapel Ministers. It was all a great turmoil, characterised no doubt by a good deal of disorder and, one suspects, some irregularity. There was also much speculation regarding the choice of Moderator of Assembly. The chair the previous year had been occupied by Dr Welsh, strong supporter of the Evangelicals, and he would have to open the proceedings, but who was to have to succeed him? From which side would the new Moderator come?

Separation

The Assembly met on 18th May and I quote from Buchanan's *Ten Years' Conflict*:

> *As the morning wore on the crowded state of the leading streets, and the look of excitement and expectation which appeared on almost every countenance must have betrayed even to the most ignorant and careless observer the approach of some great event.*

The Marquis of Bute, as Lord High Commissioner, began the day by holding a levee in the Palace of Holyroodhouse whose throne-room was crowded to suffocation. Directly opposite to where the High Commissioner stood there hung a portrait of King William III. In the general crowding against the wall this portrait became detached from its moorings and fell to the floor with a clash. In the momentary hush which followed a voice was heard saying, 'There goes the Revolution Settlement!' It couldn't have been more dramatic had it been deliberately stage-managed.

From the levee commissioners proceeded to St Giles' where the retiring Moderator, Dr Welsh, preached a sermon from the text, 'Let every man be persuaded in his own mind'. He warned, 'The controversy that has so long disturbed our Church and country is at last to be brought to an issue'.

It was afternoon before the commissioners found their way into St Andrew's Church where the Assembly was due to meet. I again quote from Buchanan:

> *The central area of the Church, allotted to members of Assembly, was already filled. The rest of the building, from the floor to the roof, presented one living mass which left no available spot unoccupied within the walls. When the Lord High Commissioner appeared Dr Welsh bowed to him and having said the usual short prayer went on to say that in view of certain events he must protest against proceeding further. He then read the protest signed by 203 members, laid it on the table, bowed to the Commissioner, stepped down from the dais and left the Church, followed by Chalmers, Candlish and others in vast numbers, so that there was now plenty of room in a hall that had been so crowded.*

The Disruption was now a fact of history.

Those who had gone out marched in solemn procession to Canonmills in the north of the city where a hall capable of accommodating three hundred people had been procured and prepared. On arrival here Dr Welsh resumed the chair, immediately proposing that Dr Thomas Chalmers be appointed Moderator, a proposal that met with tumultuous approval. Dr Chalmers then addressed the gathering in solemn and sober terms, reminding them that while there was cause for rejoicing at the freedom they had won they must maintain a deep sense of humility – 'Let him that thinketh he standeth take heed lest he fall.'

The meeting then appointed two Clerks, agreed that all who had already signed or who were ready to sign the protest were commissioners, as well as an Elder from each adhering Kirk Session. Having thus constituted the Assembly they got on with business as usual if it could be so described.

Meantime in St Andrew's Church, once the uproar had subsided, that Assembly went ahead with its business. It was noted that the Seceders had left before the court was constituted, so this deficiency was made good. Principal Haldane of St Andrews was invited to take the chair, the roll was made up, Principal McFarlane of Glasgow was elected Moderator, the commission of the Lord High was received as was the letter from Her Majesty, and generally affairs proceeded. But not quite along normal lines, for steps had to be taken to recall some recent legislation declared illegal and arrangements had to be made to provide for the care of all the parishes that had suddenly become vacant.

Two comments may be offered. First that while it might have been possible – though certainly not easy – to patch up the differences of 1843

over the power of the civil courts, it is very doubtful whether a division between the two parties
within the Kirk could have been avoided for
long. And second, one wonders whether it would
have been worthwhile avoiding the separation.
However, there can be no possible denying that
it brought much blessings for a great wave of
new life swept through the witness of the Kirk –
of both Kirks – at a time when it was urgently
and desperately needed. Truly God works in a
mysterious way.

44
WHAT WAS THE
FREE CHURCH CASE?

THERE were in fact two cases heard conjointly
in the House of Lords in 1904 (first the General
Assembly of the Free Church of Scotland,
Bannatyne and Others *versus* Lord Overtoun and
Others, and second McAlister and Others *versus*
Young and Another), but basically the contest
was one between the newly formed United Free
Church of Scotland (1900) and that part of the
Free Church which had not come into the
Union ('the Wee Frees') and the issue was
ownership of property. What, briefly, the Free
Church asked the Court to find was

> ... that the said United Free Church of Scotland
> has no right, title or interest in the lands, property
> or funds held for the Free Church prior to the
> Union and that those adhering to the Free Church
> lawfully represent the said Free Church and are
> entitled to have the whole of the said lands, property
> and funds applied according to the terms of the
> trusts upon which they are respectfully held, and
> their successors.

Judgment was given in favour of the Free Church.

As can readily be imagined the case had a history, its judgment had a sequel, and it itself raises issues of profound importance and interest – so much so that 76 closely packed pages are required to record their Lordships' findings.

History

Just how their heritable properties should be held had always presented something of a problem for the non-established Churches. The property of the Church of Scotland was attached to it by statute, but there being no such provision in the case of the various breakaway groups it was necessary for title to property to be taken in name of trustees and therefore to be governed by the general Law of Trust. When a dispute relative to property came before the courts, therefore, the exercise involved was in essence one of interpreting trust purposes, and however straightforward this may sound it can, in case of a religious body, be far from simple.

Obviously in the eighteenth century, when congregations were splitting and splitting again, questions were bound to be constantly arising about the right to the buildings. The standard situation was that a group had been received, say, as a congregation of the Associate Synod. Money had been subscribed to make it possible to have a meeting-house built and this was vested in trustees for behoof of the congregation – or was it for behoof of the cause? So long as the congregation plodded along faithfully within the ranks of the Associate Synod, the question remained one of purely academic interest. But when trouble broke out over, say, the New Light controversy and a minority broke away waving the Auld Licht banner, there was a problem, for it could be argued that it was they and they alone who represented the purpose for which the money had been given. On the other hand, if it was congregational property surely the majority should prevail.

One very famous case was that of Craigdallie which was in and out of the courts for twenty years before concluding with a House of Lords judgment based on the principle that 'property is held in trust for the principles of the Church'. This had two important implications. For one thing it means that in the exercise of its freedom to formulate and interpret its own standards any denomination will be greatly hampered by the thought that in accepting change in its basic principles it may well be putting its property at risk. And for another it means that the civil courts, which it is universally agreed are the appropriate authority to administer Trust Law, are going to find themselves having to interpret abstruse theological principles, matters that are wholly spiritual in character.

This was the situation in 1904 when the Free Church Case reached the House of Lords.

The Case

In 1900 the Free Church and the United Presbyterian Church came together to form the United Free Church of Scotland. It was unfortunate that a small but healthy minority on the Free Church side stayed out of the union, continuing as the Free Church. Generally known today as the 'Wee Frees' the thirty congregations concerned were situated mainly in the Highlands and Islands. The Ministers of this minority were deposed by the united body and actions were raised against them to have them evicted from the property they were occupying. The Free Church responded with an action to recover all the property and funds that had been theirs at the date of union. Hence the conjoint cases.

The Free Church case was based on the simple claim that those of their number who had gone into the union had been able to do so only by renouncing Free Church principles, having done so in two important particulars. For one thing they had departed from the tenet, basic and dear to the Free Church, that there should be a National Establishment of Religion. This they had cast aside in favour of a voluntaryism that came from the Secession; for another, in no longer holding as a creed the Westminster Confession of Faith in its entirety, and in requiring from each Minister and Elder at ordination a declaration of his belief that the whole doctrine of the Confession was the truth of God, and that he would constantly adhere thereto.

Many days were spent in pleading and many more in avizandum. Indeed because of the death of Lord Shand before he had signed his judgment, the whole case had to heard a second time. By a majority of five to two the court found in favour of the Free Kirk.

The Sequel

Rarely can a judgment have caused more widespread alarm or threatened greater havoc. The thirty congregations of the Free Kirk had suddenly acquired enormous property resources which they had not the ability to administer, nor the funds to maintain, nor the need to use. Rarely can there have been a situation where the phrase 'embarrassment of riches' more aptly applied. And if the Wee Free were in a sore plight through owning too much, the United Free Church was in a quite terrifying situation. More than half of their congregations throughout Scotland had become homeless, and with their central funds desperately depleted their future appeared bleak indeed.

So serious – or should one say, ridiculous – was the position that the following year Parliament intervened to the extent of appointing a Commission to allocate the property on a fair and equitable basis. Among the title-papers of most of the property of Free Church congregations now in the Church of Scotland, there will be found an Act of Allocation transferring property of the Free Church to the congregation in question – an allocation gained after submitting and supporting a claim before the Commission. The lawyers must have had a wonderful time.

To a simple soul unversed in such matters it may seem a sad if interesting commentary on our legal system that a judgment reached by our supreme court of law had to be followed by the appointment of a Commission to ensure that in spite of the said judgment some semblance of justice was achieved.

45
WHAT WAS THE UNION OF 1929?

FROM 1740 until 1843 the Kirk in Scotland had known incident after incident of secession and division, once and again a group had broken away from the main body, only itself very soon to be splintered into smaller groups. Today we incline to condemn such happenings and to attribute them to sheer thrawnness on the part of our forefathers. We should remember, though, that Presbyterianism is a system which treasures very dearly the freedom of the individual, recognising each man's responsibility for his own soul, and we have to realise that you cannot at one and the same time burden a man with the duty of satisfying himself of the truth of his creed and require of him implicit obedience to the dictates of an infallible Church.

It was not all that long after the Disruption in 1843, there was seen a quite tangible token of a movement towards reconciliation in which it seemed possible that some of the ancient sores might be healed and that the divided robe might be knit together again. But, of course, it was not until 1929 that this movement reached its fulfilment and culmination in the union of the Church of Scotland with the United Free Church of Scotland – an historic event which took place in Edinburgh on 2nd October 1929 – now usually referred to as 'the Union of 1929'.

Moving closer together

As early as 1870 the Church of Scotland had publicly expressed a 'hearty willingness and desire to take all possible steps consistent with the principles on which the Church was founded to promote the reunion of Churches having a common origin, adhering to the same Confession of faith and the same system of government and worship'. But it was not until nearly forty years later that a Committee was appointed to seek ways and means of furthering the cause of union with the United Free Church. In these intervening years many influences had been at work.

For one thing the specific issue which had led to the Disruption had lost all its significance when in 1874 Parliament agreed to the complete abolition of all patronage within the Church of Scotland. For its part the Free Church had come to see, as a result of the Cardross Case (and later still the Free Church case) that any Church, however much it may claim to be free in matters spiritual, is very much dependant for the maintenance of that very freedom upon the law of the land and the courts which administer it.

For another thing the union of the former Free and UP Churches in 1900 had proved a complete success, had shown what could be done, and had achieved softening of some of the more extreme doctrines of voluntaryism. The creation within the Church of Scotland of so many new parishes *quoad sacra* had brought all the congregations of the two denominations more closely towards one pattern in constitution and government.

However clearly the principles that had led to separation might be cherished by leaders and historians, the ordinary Church member was coming to think less of these and more of the great things held in common – the same Bible, the same Psalms and Hymns, the same type of worship, the same Sunday Schools and Bible Classes. When a family moved to a new district they might well change from one denomination to another, on marriage one partner joined the congregation of the other without thought of sacrifice or of apostasy. And, of course, this tendency gained fresh impetus during the Great War when men at the front attended the one service and women at home prayed together. There is nothing to equal shared danger for breaking down walls of partition.

Obstacles in the Way

There were, however, particularly in the opinion of the United Free Church, certain obstacles blocking the way towards union. First there was the old question of how far an established Church could really be free. The adoption by Parliament in 1921 of the Articles Declaratory of the Constitution of the Church of Scotland went far to meet this difficulty. On the one hand it satisfied the upholders of the idea of freedom by showing clearly that the Church stood in no position of subservience to the State, and on the other hand it met the needs of the defenders of establishment who were convinced that much good had come of the close relationship of Church and State and were determined that nothing of this was to be lost. Of that Act it was said at the time by an eminent authority that it 'harmonises with a definiteness and completeness for which I think no parallel in Christian history is to be found the National Recognition of Religion with the Spiritual Freedom of the Church'.

The other main difficulty had to do with the endowments of the Church of Scotland and with its heritable property. In this connection the UF Church had made it a condition of union 'that all the endowments of the Church of Scotland must be vested in it under a tenure which is consistent with the freedom set forth in the Articles and which recognises no right of the State to exercise any special control over the Church in virtue of its enjoyment of these endowments'. The needs of this situation were met by the passing of the Church of Scotland (Property and Endowments Act of 1925) which vested in the General Trustees churches, manses and glebes, as well as all rights in stipend – these to be the absolute property of the Church in all time coming.

The Act of Union

So it was that the objections were met and the difficulties surmounted. On 1st October 1929 the two Assemblies met in their own separate meeting-places. On the following day they moved, each from its own hall, to mingle at the top of Bank Street and walk side by side to St Giles' for a solemn Service of Union. Then in the afternoon they met, 1200 of them (the largest indoor gathering ever to congregate in Edinburgh) in a huge garage, and while showers of hail beat upon the glass roof, agreed to a Basis of Union that was once again after close on two hundred years to make possible the united witness of a great National Church in Scotland.

More than any other single individual Dr John White deserves the name of Architect of the Union of 1929. It may be fitting, then, to close by quoting from his speech at that first Assembly:

We must make our thanksgiving to God, who has guided the Union movement, bringing the Churches in these late years steadily in the direction of this later fellowship. Very humbly, very reverently, and with deep gratitude we acknowledge and believe that it is He alone who has brought us to this hour of realised hope, of answered prayer, and of fervent desires fulfilled. And now that the seal has been set to the solemn covenant declaring the Churches no longer twain but one our first act of thanksgiving is to consecrate ourselves anew to the service of our Lord and Saviour, humbly acknowledging our entire dependence on the mercy of God and the leading of His Holy Spirit for all the happy issues we look for in the coming days.

To which we all say Amen.